The Stars, the Snow, the Fire

Other Books by John Haines

The Stars, the Snow, the Fire

A MEMOIR BY

John Haines

Twenty-Five Years in the Northern Wilderness

Graywolf Press

SAINT PAUL, MINNESOTA

Publication of this volume is made possible in part by a grant provided by the Minnesota State Arts Board through an appropriation by the Minnesota State Legislature, and by a grant from the National Endowment for the Arts. Significant support has also been provided by the Bush Foundation; Dayton's, Mervyn's, and Target stores through the Dayton Hudson Foundation; the McKnight Foundation; and other generous contributions from foundations, corporations, and individuals. To these organizations and individuals we offer our heartfelt thanks.

Support for this edition has been provided, in part, by a twenty-fifth anniversary donation to Graywolf from founder Scott Walker in honor of Chris Faatz, Kathleen Foster, Sam Hammill, Sheila Murphy, Jim Sitter, Tree Swenson, John Taylor, Patt Wagoner, and Joe Wheeler.

The essays collected in this book have appeared previously in the following publications: *Alaska Airlines Magazine, Anchorage Daily News, Antaeus, Harper's, Homer News* (Alaska), *Ironwood, Kansas Quarterly, The Living Wilderness, Montana Review, Nature Conservancy News, New England Review, Permafrost,* and *ZYZZYVA.* Also in previous books and chapbooks: *Of Traps and Snares* (1981), *Other Days* (1982), *The Graywolf Annual Three* (1986), and *Stories We Listened To* (1986).

Published by Graywolf Press
2402 University Avenue, Suite 203
Saint Paul, Minnesota 55114
All rights reserved.

www.graywolfpress.org

Published in the United States of America

ISBN 1-55597-306-X

2 4 6 8 9 7 5 3 1
First Graywolf Printing, 2000

Library of Congress Catalog Card Number: 99-067945

Cover design: Julie Metz
Cover photograph: © Tom Bean/Tony Stone Images

Table of Contents

The 'truest' thing about the experience is now neither that it was from hour to hour thus and so; nor is it my fairly accurate 'memory' of how it was from hour to hour in chronological progression; but rather as it turns up in recall in no such order, casting its lights and associations forward and backward upon the then past and the then future.

— JAMES AGEE

AL VERO LETTORE

Preface

I N ITSELF, CHRONOLOGY IS SELDOM A satisfactory guide to the events of one's life, and in the present case is even less so. My time in the Far North amounts to both more and less than twenty-five years. It has been forty-two years now since I first settled at Richardson in the summer of 1947; I remained there only until late August of the following year. The longest and most active period of residence was hardly more than a dozen additional years—from 1954 until the late 1960s. We can add to this that for the past eight years I have again lived at Richardson, though with extended periods of absence. So that what is implied in a subtitle is at best a symbolic figure that stands for many arrivals and departures.

The actual writing of these pages has occurred long after the events, and mostly in other places: in California, Seattle, Montana, and the north of England. In reliving parts of the narrative, I seem to have wandered through a number of historical periods, geological epochs, and states of mind, always returning to a source, a country that is both specific and ideal. Perhaps, then, as much as it is about anything else, this book is about Time—one's sense of time, and the time in which certain events take place. This journey in and out of time cannot be adequately expressed by any sum of calendar years. In the sense in which I write, there is no progress, no destination, for the essence of things has already been known, the real place arrived at long ago.

More than one reader of these essays and chapters has remarked on the dreamlike quality of many of the episodes. I think I have always been aware of certain events as existing in a kind of *dream-time* in the ancient tribal sense of this. When, at one point in the narrative, I say that it was all "far, far back in time," this is not merely a rhetorical figure. For somehow those days in the field, those treks with the dogs over snow and grass, the long hunts, the animal killing, and the rest of it, were all part of the inmost human experience on this earth. That experience is still valid if anything is. Its energies can be translated into many fields and activities, but the heart of it remains constant and true.

It is true also that certain experiences, states of mind, and ways of life, cannot be willed back. That intuitive relation to the world we shared with animals, with everything that exists, once out-grown, rarely returns in all its convincing power. Observation, studies in the field, no matter how acute and exhaustive, cannot replace it, for the experience cannot be reduced to abstractions, for-mulas, and explanations. It is rank, it smells of blood and killed meat, is compounded of fear, of danger and delight in unequal measure. To the extent that it can even be called "experience" and not by some other, forgotten name, it requires a surrender few of us now are willing to make. Yet, in the brief clarity and intensity of an encounter with nature, in the act of love, and (since we are con-cerned with a book) in the recalling and retelling of a few elemental episodes, certain key moments in that experience can be regained. On these depends the one vitality of life without which no art, no spiritual definition, no true relation to the world is possible.

JOHN HAINES, *February 1989*

John Haines at the Richardson Homestead, September 1980

The Stars, the Snow, the Fire

Snow

To one who lives in the snow and watches it day by day, it is a book to be read. The pages turn as the wind blows; the characters shift and the images formed by their combinations change in meaning, but the language remains the same. It is a shadow language, spoken by things that have gone by and will come again. The same text has been written there for thousands of years, though I was not here, and will not be here in winters to come, to read it. These seemingly random ways, these paths, these beds, these footprints, these hard, round pellets in the snow: they all have meaning. Dark things may be written there, news of other lives, their sorties and excursions, their terrors and deaths. The tiny feet of a shrew or a vole make a brief, erratic pattern across the snow, and here is a hole down which the animal goes. And now the track of an ermine comes this way, swift and searching, and he too goes down that white shadow of a hole.

A wolverine, and the loping, toed-in track I followed uphill for two miles one spring morning, until it finally dropped away into another watershed and I gave up following it. I wanted to see where he would go and what he would do. But he just went on, certain of where he was going, and nothing came of it for me to see but that sure and steady track in the snowcrust, and the sunlight strong in my eyes.

Snow blows across the highway before me as I walk—little, wavering trails of it swept along like a people dispersed. The snow people—where are they going? Some great danger must pursue them. They hurry and fall; the wind gives them a push, they get up and go on again.

I was walking home from Redmond Creek one morning late in January. On a divide between two watersheds I came upon the scene of a battle between a moose and three wolves. The story was written plainly in the snow at my feet. The wolves had come in from the west, following an old trail from the Salcha River, and had found the moose feeding in an open stretch of the overgrown road I was walking.

The sign was fresh, it must have happened the night before. The snow was torn up, with chunks of frozen moss and broken sticks scattered about; here and there, swatches of moose hair. A confusion of tracks in the trampled snow—the splayed, stabbing feet of the moose, the big, furred pads and spread toenails of the wolves.

I walked on, watching the snow. The moose was large and alone, almost certainly a bull. In one place he backed himself into a low, brush-hung bank to protect his rear. The wolves moved away from him—those moose feet are dangerous. The moose turned, ran on for fifty yards, and the fight began again. It became a running, broken fight that went on for nearly half a mile in the changing, rutted terrain, the red morning light coming across the hills from the sun low in the south. A pattern shifting and uncertain; the wolves relenting, running out into the brush in a wide circle, and closing again: another patch of moose hair in the trodden snow.

I felt that I knew those wolves. I had seen their tracks several times before during that winter, and once they had taken a marten from one of my traps. I believed them to be a female and two nearly grown pups. If I was right, she may have been teaching them how to hunt, and all that turmoil in the snow may have been the serious play of things that must kill to live. But I saw no blood sign that morning, and the moose seemed to have gotten the better of the fight. At the end of it he plunged away into thick alder brush. I saw his tracks, moving more slowly now, as he climbed through a low saddle, going north in the shallow, unbroken snow. The three wolves trotted east toward Banner Creek.

What might have been silence, an unwritten page, an absence, spoke to me as clearly as if I had been there to see it. I have imagined a man who might live as the coldest scholar on earth, who followed each clue in the snow, writing a book as he went. It would be the history of snow, the book of winter. A thousand-year text to be read by a people hunting these hills in a distant time. Who was here, and who has gone? What were their names? What did they kill and eat? Whom did they leave behind?

Of Traps and Snares

THE LORE OF TRAPS AND SNARES. The old handbooks are filled with talk of lures and sets and skills. The subject has its own fascination, and to one attracted to life in the woods this knowledge seems essential and good, something handed down, useful, and binding in time. The world may fail us, the markets crash, and the traffic stand still. But with a good axe in hand, a gun, a net, a few traps—life will go on in the old, upstanding ways.

If we don't have steel traps, and are otherwise cut off from the tools of commerce, we can always make deadfalls. Men made them in early days when hardware was scarce and expensive; they made them out of whatever the country provided, from logs and stones. Abandoned, these native materials soon fell to rot and were added to the soil and covered with snow. Steel cable and copper wire can also be done without. When white men first came into the country, late in the century, they found the Indians catching marten and rabbits and other small animals in snares made from sinew, or from strands of halibut twine they had gotten from traders on the coast.

The plain vocabulary of this woodlore hardly conceals a native harshness. Sooner or later the thinking man considers the barbaric means for what is plainly a kind of murder: the steel jaw and the wire noose, the choking and the crushing, the cutting and tearing of the wet skin from the cold body of the dead beast. And the end in view: selling the fur so that others may be rich and clothed beyond their natural right.

In all that hardness and cruelty there is a knowledge to be

gained, a necessary knowledge, acquired in the only way it can be, from close familiarity with the creatures hunted. A knowledge of blood, of sinew and gut; of the structure of joint and muscle, the shape of the skull, the angularity, the sharpness or roundness of nose and ears and lips and teeth. There is passion in the hand that pulls the pelt and strokes the fur, confident that it knows as second nature all the hinges and recesses of the animal body. But however close that familiarity, something is always withheld; the life of the animal remains other and beyond, never completely yielding all that it is.

So much can be said about it from one conviction or another, the attitudes easily become partisan and intractible. There is the coarseness too often found in those who follow the trade, especially where mere cash is the end in mind. And yet to some fortunate individuals there have been few things more deeply attractive than this seasonal pursuit of the wild. It is life at its fullest, uncertain and demanding, but rich with expectation. The wilderness is open, and whoever enters it knows the satisfaction of being at ease in a country he calls his own. The land belongs to him and to no one else. He can go where he likes, following his own trail through the spruce bogs and across the dry birch hills, a pathway tramped in the snow, to stop at nightfall in his own snug camp.

It will never be an easy life, the gift comes with its hardships firmly attached: the occasional poor season and bad luck, the missed hunt, the weariness and disappointment; long days alone in the snow and frost with no sure reward for the time spent. Some things make sense only in the light of their personal necessity, and what that necessity is to be we choose for ourselves.

I ran a trapline periodically for over twenty years in interior Alaska. That old, persistent dream, fed by the old tales, the worn books: to be alone in the snow with my dogs, tending the traps and snares. The trail before me, and the life of the animals I sought, secret and apart from my own.

It was part of the homestead life there at Richardson, on the bluff hills above the Tanana River east of Fairbanks. It was something else to do, and at times it brought in that small amount of money we needed. But it was in some ways an unlucky time to be a trapper; fur prices were low, and for most of those years the country hadn't much fur in it.

My first winter alone in the cabin at Richardson, when I was still in my twenties and knew nothing at all about living in the North, I went out with an older neighbor named Fred Allison one afternoon in November to set snares for rabbits. Allison was that increasingly rare survivor from early days, having mined and teamstered, driven mail, trapped and roughnecked his forty-odd years in the North. Now he was tending bar in the roadhouse at Richardson two miles down the road. From behind the counter he watched me with his one good eye, curious how I, a quiet and uncertain youth from the city, was finding my way in a new country. While I did occasional chores for him and we met from time to time in conversation, he would tell me things that he knew and that he thought would be good for me to learn. And now he was going to show me, convinced, perhaps, that I would never learn otherwise. He had spent his own young days in the woods in eastern Canada, and knew what it was to live on rabbits and grouse when nothing else was on hand. Nearly seventy, limping and slow in his walk, I think he was glad in his last, lame years to have something to do outside the tame routine he had come to, feeding coal to the kitchen range, answering the gas pump bell and waiting on infrequent customers in the bar.

We went down into the woods below the roadhouse, toward the river. It was growing late in a dry fall, the ground was frozen, and a few inches of grainy snow bent down the small grasses and lay thinly on the moss. There were plenty of rabbits that winter, and their trails were beaten through the willows and birches; a maze of neighborhood pathways crossing and interrupting each other, and to the unskilled eye going nowhere at all.

We tramped around in the woods, while Fred swore and muttered to himself, half-confiding to me some of the secrets of rabbit-snaring. Finally he chose a place, an opening in the willows where a rabbit path was confined by the brush around it. As I stood aside and watched him, he found a dead willow standing nearby, broke from it a section about three feet long and stripped it of branches. It should be dry rather than green, he explained in a voice indefinably Scots or Nova Scotian, "Because, you see, your rabbit might stop to nibble the green stick, and he wouldn't go into the snare."

We had brought with us a few lengths of thin copper wire. Fred took a piece of the wire, and in one end of it he made a sliding noose, three inches or so in diameter. He wound the other end of the wire midway on the stick and made it tight. Then, kneeling down in the snow beside the path and disturbing the ground as little as possible, he carefully worked the stick into the brush above the rabbit path, so that it was fixed firmly there, the noose hanging down a few inches above the snow. Explaining with a word or two what he was doing—"Now you see . . ." He arranged other dry sticks around the snare, on either side and above it, and two small stubs beneath it. Satisfied, he got to his feet with a grunt, and we both stood and looked at the snare.

There was only one way through that opening now. A rabbit would come in the night and find its way partly blocked. The chances were that it would not go back, but put its head into the snare, try to go on, and be caught, to choke and freeze in a short time. The colder it was, the better. But you had to be careful about the way you did it. The snare must be short enough that the rabbit could not turn easily when caught and bite the wire. Sometimes one of them would get a foot into a carelessly set snare, and eventually break the wire and get away.

Soon enough I saw how it was done, standing beside Allison in the snow, while his strongly hooked red nose dripped snot, and the cold, grey dusk deepened around us. "There now, my boy," he said, pleased with what he had done. "Come back in the morning, and you'll find a rabbit!"

We set four or five snares that afternoon, all within a small space of ground where the rabbit sign was thickest. It was nearly dark when we walked out of the woods to the roadhouse for supper. When I came back the following day, sure enough, I found two rabbits frozen in the snares. They were bunched up in the torn brush, contorted, feet in the air, their eyes turned to ice.

From then on, whenever I wanted a rabbit, for myself or for my dogs, I went out and set a few snares. But it wasn't always as easily done as that first time. As long as the rabbits were abundant no great cunning was needed to catch them. But when they were scarce they seemed to become cagey and shy. They would stop and go back, or find some way around the snare rather than go through it. Great numbers made them careless, or they were too busy chasing each other in the dark to notice the wire.

There was a fox in the neighborhood then. We saw him sometimes from the roadhouse when he came up from the river at dusk to hunt rabbits in the birchwood. One evening when I went down to look at my snares, I met the fox in my trail. I saw him coming across an open field beyond the woods, his dark red form stepping surely and alertly through the clumps of snow-covered grasses. I stopped and stood quietly where I was, half in among the trees. The fox did not see me, but trotted to within five feet of me before he caught my scent and crouched down on the snowpath, uncertain. Suddenly his big yellow eyes blazed up at me, and he turned and fled.

I caught that fox in a trap a few weeks later. It was my first attempt. I followed Allison's advice, using a fresh piece of rabbit for bait. I set the trap carefully in the snow at the base of a large spruce tree near where the fox had been hunting, and covered it with a thin sheet of paper. The trap chain with its chunk of dead wood for a drag was concealed in the snow beside it. I sprinkled some fresh snow around the set to cover my tracks, and left it there for several days. I came back one mild, sunlit afternoon to find the fox caught fast in the trap by one of its hind legs. He had not run far, but was still tugging on the chain where it had tangled in the brush, trying to get free. The skin of his caught leg was broken and bloody, and his eyes had a baffled and wounded look.

What to do. Allison had told me how to kill him. I was not to shoot him, for that would make a hole in the skin and diminish its value. The best way was to knock him out with a sharp blow across the bridge of his nose. While he was unconscious I should grab him and break his neck. Allison told me how. I was skeptical and a little afraid, but I was also determined to learn.

I found a stout, dry stick in the willows around me; the fox was backed into the brush, silently watching me. I got myself close enough, reached out with my stick, and hit him a good rap in what I thought was the right place. To my surprise, but just as Allison said he would, the fox suddenly stiffened and fell.

He would not stay that way long, so I quickly kneeled down in the snow. I seized the unconscious fox by his forelegs and drew him into my lap. Holding him there with one hand, I grasped his muzzle tightly in my other hand and twisted his head as far around as I could, until I felt the neck bone snap, and a sudden gush of blood came from his nostrils. A shudder ran through the slender, furred body, and then it was still.

I released him and got to my feet. I stood there, looking down at the soiled, limp form in the snow, appalled at what I had done. This is what trapping meant when all the romance was removed from it: a matter of deceit and steel set against hunger. But I had overcome my fear, and I felt something had been gained by that.

For the rest of that winter I set a trap only now and then. I worked on my cabin, mended clothing, and read the few books I had with me. I spent many hours visiting the older residents with whom I became friendly, listening to their tales of works and days. As spring came on and heavy snow came to the hills, I went out on my snowshoes, roaming ever wider into the country, taking more and deeper note of the woods around me and all that would become the ground of my life.

I left Richardson the following fall, after another summer of clearing and building. For a time I was back in the world of cities and people, of books and schools—another part of the forest with its own snares and deceptions. I returned early one May with a young wife, resolved now to live the homestead life as fully as I could. I was thirty years old, and I found my world again, house, yard, and wilderness, more or less as I had left it. Allison had moved away, retired to the State of Washington, and the road-house had new owners. The road to Fairbanks had been straightened and paved in my absence, and there were a few new settlers on the road out from town; but the Tanana River and the country to the north and south of us had not changed, still unsurveyed, quiet, and empty of people.

It was a good time to be in the woods, one of those periodic years of abundance in the North. The rabbits were thick, at the peak of their cycle, and everything else in the woods was bound to flourish. We came upon lynx everywhere we went, in the hills and in the swamps. There were big ones, small ones, females with kittens. The sheer richness of it was astonishing. Rabbits bounded away underfoot, and the big, tawny grey lynx seemed nearly as tame as tabbies; they moved deliberately across the trails and through the clearings, or sat blinking by the roadside in the evenings, as if they were stunned by the abundance of food. That winter Fred Campbell, one of the old Richardson trappers, caught fifty lynx in snares, and Hans Seppala across the Tanana caught another forty-five or fifty in traps. That was a lot of fur animals to take out of one country, but Campbell justified it, claiming that in a year or so the big cats would be gone anyway, starved and eating each other when the rabbits died off.

Two years later there was hardly a lynx left in the country and scarcely a rabbit to be found. When I took up trapping again, determined to make it a serious part of my life, it was at the poorest time in a decade. Poverty gripped the woods, and when the fall snow came there was nothing to be seen in it but a few squirrel tracks, or now and then an ermine or mouse-hunting fox. Even moose became scarce for a while, as if they too had been driven by some great famine to a farther country.

I was alone then for the most part, marriage and the wilderness having come to their parting. I had myself, four dogs, a couple of sleds, harness and snowshoes, a few books, and a passion for the country. I set out to learn what I could and prepare myself for a long life in the woods.

For a time I set my traps along the Tanana and in the old roads around Richardson and Tenderfoot, within easy miles of home. Very little immediate reward came of all my walking and searching, a perplexed peering into the snow. But I was schooled all the same. I learned to read animal sign, the snowmark of foot and tail and wing. In some uncanny and prehuman way it was like beginning a new language, each detail and accent of which had its special meaning. It led me step by step into a world I seemed to have known once but had forgotten, shadowy and haunted by half-realized images from the past. I found my way there, somehow assured, though alone and separated from all I had grown up with, that I was in my right place, performing the right tasks.

Now and then I caught an ermine or a fox. I snared a big lynx in one of my foot trails near the river. I tried to catch rabbits again as I had once done so easily, setting my snares wherever I found a solitary track. But the country proved to be barren of fur, and I saw that no amount of time and work would change that. I realized that I would have to go much farther and find another country away from the river and the highway.

I hung up my traps for a season or two. Working in the fall and in the spring, when I had time and the days were longer, I began building a system of trails and camps in the only country available to me then, the boggy creeks and spruce ridges northwest of Richardson. This was the Redmond Creek country, draining west from the Banner watershed; it was higher and wetter than home, and dominated by the broad height of Banner Dome, a bare and windy summit from which you could look down into the Salcha River drainage and north toward the Yukon itself. It was a country deeply marked by the overgrown trails and wagon roads of the gold rush, and walking these for any distance I was sure to come sooner or later on a fallen cabin or the partly cribbed remains of a prospect hole with a rotting ladder standing there in the brush as if ready for use. The country had been partially burned over, hunted over, and trapped over during those hectic and destructive years, and it was never really rich in game and fur afterwards. But there were moose in it now, undisturbed by hunters, and always a few marten on the ridges and a rare lynx prowling the willow thickets in the creek bottoms.

Surveying this country by foot and snowshoe, chopping and blazing, plotting and building, I made for myself a personal domain of which I was the sole ruler and working occupant. By the time I was done with it, or as much done as one ever is with such things in the woods, I could claim at least thirty miles of trail laid out north, east, and west along the ridges and benches. Much of this was cut wide and straight enough to take the sled and dogs, with here and there a roughly blazed footpath striking off into some part of the country where I found it necessary to go. I put a lot of care into making those trails, and I take some pride in knowing that most of them are still there, sound and true. A trail through the woods is made for a purpose; and if it is important enough it is worth the time spent to do it well—or so I thought as I sighted a way through the birches to the next rise, and checked behind me to see that the way was clear and the grade as easy as I could make it.

With daily and seasonal use these trails became in their own essential way a part of the homestead, an extension of the yard. As naturally as leaves falling, came the inevitable places to rest while traveling, to view the hills or to look for a moose; favorite clearings, windfalls to gather firewood from, patches in which to pick blueberries and cranberries. All things encountered along a trail might be of use—a dry snag for kindling, a dead birch for the bark that held it upright, a dry leaf floor under aspens for a crop of mushrooms in late summer. In no time at all the trails acquired their home legend of past kills and other memorable events—here a bear was feeding early in the summer, and there last fall a bull moose stripped a spruce sapling of its branches with his horns. There were caches built in the trees, items placed for use at a later time, tent poles and berry buckets. By the stream-crossings and waterholes I left tin cans upside down in the brush to use for a drinking cup on hot summer days. In a few seasons the country became worn and familiar like a neighborhood, though spread over many miles of birch hills, alder thickets, and black spruce bogs. The trails were hard going in places, the ground wet, the summer-thawed moss exhausting to walk over, and the hills sometimes long and steep, but it was my own made place. The labor of it occupied me the better part of three years, but I have known and done few things more satisfying. I contemplated the map with a sure sense that I knew where I was in that far corner of North America.

I had no competitors in all that country. There were few people trapping anywhere in those years, and around Richardson only two of the old, dedicated, and solitary kind were left. Hans Seppala kept to himself in the flat Clearwater country across the Tanana where he had been for the better part of thirty years, his only access to the world a riverboat in the summer and a dog team in the winter. Fred Campbell owned the hills northeast of Richardson, but his trapping days were at an end; the big year of the lynx had been his last, and he took a meager solace in his memories. When he died late one fall toward the end of the 1950s I considered taking over his old trapline and adding it to my own. We had talked about it once or twice, skirting what was for him the painful admission that he could not keep it any longer. But he wanted money for what he had, and I had none to give him. There was not much left of it by then, in any case—two tumbledown cabins, some rusty traps, and the forty to fifty miles of trails he had maintained for nearly forty years, away north behind Buckeye Dome, and all the way to McCoy Creek on the Salcha drainage. It was good marten country, remote, and uninhabited by any other trapper; but the distance was greater than I wanted to travel, and by then I was well into my own territory. It would be enough.

To make the most of this widespread country I had two choices. One was to build cabins, more or less permanent camps at convenient distances, though each of these might occupy part of a summer's work. The other was to brave the cold and camp in the open under a canvas lean-to or in a small tent. This was not always the extreme hardship it might appear to be, though at thirty and forty below zero it was always an adventure. If nothing else it toughened one for the life and made the encounter with the wilderness just that much closer and deeper. But after a few experiences camping in the cold, in a worn eight-by-ten-foot wall tent with a sheet-iron stove, sleeping out, or "siwashing," as it used to be called, I chose to build a cabin, both for the comfort of it and for the sense of a permanent place that it gave me.

Along the way I rebuilt two ancient and disused cabins left behind many years before by old residents in the country. One of these was a tiny square hut of a thing with a dirt floor and sod roof on a low bluff near the mouth of Tenderfoot Creek, six miles upriver from the homestead. Although it was too small to be more than a temporary camp, for three or four years it was useful to me as a fishing camp and as a shelter while trapping. The other cabin, tilted and barely standing when I found it, was in Issacson Flat, a few miles up Banner Creek and over a long steep hill from home. I patched up these two camps, furnishing each of them with a bunk and a stove, a few pots and dishes. They would be there with a rick or two of firewood, available to me at the end of a long day if I needed them. But I used these two camps only now and then, and the country around them was seldom good for trapping.

And then one rainy fall my second wife and I built a small, snug cabin on a wet bench above one of the creeks that drained off Banner Dome, several miles north of the homestead. We worked three hard months building that place; the rain turned into snow, and the bark froze to the timber before the roof was on, but it was worth it. The cabin, with four doghouses and a meat rack, was well placed, with a good view into a grassy flat, in a good country. There were moose in the creeks and marten on the hills, the big dome above the cabin, making a high, far sound in the wind.

It is often true that the best things we do in some strange way take place within us long before we come to the ground itself. The physical domain of the country had its counterpart in me. The trails I made led outward into the hills and swamps, but they led inward also. And from the study of things underfoot, and from reading and thinking, came a kind of exploration, myself and the land. In time the two became one in my mind. With the gathering force of an essential thing realizing itself out of early ground, I faced in myself a passionate and tenacious longing—to put away thought forever, and all the trouble it brings, all but the nearest desire, direct and searching. To take the trail and not look back. Whether on foot, on snowshoes, or by sled, into the summer hills and their late-freezing shadows—a high blaze, a runner track in the snow would show where I had gone. Let the rest of mankind find me if it could.

Stopped briefly in a still fall afternoon, resting while on a hunt, I looked north from a high and open slope to another range of hills—what lay beyond them? What did I hear once of that distant and rocky prominence someone had called "The Butte"? I studied my favorite map with its legend of watersheds and old trails, its numerals and lines of elevation. The names I read there spoke to me: Caribou, Deep Creek, Deadwood, Monte Cristo. Each name, each creek, each wooded rise of ground led on to another. I might, at a long stretch of fancy, have gone all the way north to the Yukon. I would build another camp a day's travel on, and another beyond that, until I reached the great river, or as far as I wished to go.

Or, again, I could as easily turn south. I remember thinking one fall with excitement and conviction that we should go across the Tanana, into the foothills of the Alaska Range, and make another country there. No one had trapped and hunted there in recent years—think of being so close to those high ridges whose snow line we watched each fall as if we gazed into some far Tibet. There were caribou and grizzlies there, and who knows what fabulous country to roam in.

They were big and indefinite dreams never realized, though I could imagine them down to the last detail—the camps I would build, the trails I would cut, the fall hunt coming on early near timberline. But for me finally there were limits. Things at home also had their claim on me—that other world of books, and of thoughts that went far beyond such immediate things as hunting and trapping, into a country of their own. I would stay where I was and make the most of what I had.

The trapping year had its own calendar, and everything fitted a niche in the months and days. The Far North summer passed quickly, a round of gardening and berry-picking, of fishing and woodcutting—a chopping and hauling and stacking that never stopped for long under the great span of daylight. In late August darkness returned, with the glitter of frost in the mornings. Fall came on with its ice and color, with the late rush to dig potatoes and gather in the garden and greenhouse crop. The river channels shrank, the water slowly cleared of silt, and pan ice clung in the eddies. Fishing ended with the nets dried and put away, the boat hauled out on a sandbar and secured for the winter. With luck, the hunt was over and a moose was hanging in the shade. The last swans passed overhead with distant cries, and the woods were quiet.

Snow came and melted, and came again, a patchy whiteness over the fallen debris of summer. Sometime in October the first good snowfall came and remained on the ground; anything that moved upon it left its sign to be read. November came, and the snowfall deepened with the cold, falling at night far below zero. I would go for a long hike over the hills one day to look at the fur sign, or I might see while hunting late that the marten were in good number that year. At home I sorted traps and looked over snares, deciding what to do. I felt the season steady on its downward track as I paused there, weighing my choices: three months' travel in the dark, or a winter at home with my books and thoughts. The two things squared off—needs and wants. My decision to trap sometimes came almost as an afterthought. I had a moose down somewhere back in the hills, and in no time a marten or two would find it and attempt to feed on the meat while it was hanging in the woods. I set a couple of traps then and there. The signs looked good, and besides I had to come and haul the meat home, didn't I? The sled was taken from storage, the harness checked and mended. The dogs were restless.

My traps were a scattering of sizes and sorts, from the small #1 jumps I used for marten, to the larger double-spring Victor and Newhouse made for fox, for coyote and beaver. Some of these had teeth—ugly, grim-looking things that were dangerous and hard to set. I had bought a few of them out of a bin in Fairbanks once, years before I knew what I needed and wanted; others were given to me, or I found them in one place or another. They piled up, in boxes at home or hung from nails on the wall of a camp. To save myself some of the work of packing them, I often left my marten traps hanging in trees along the trail, to be used the following season. They got a little rusty there in the weather, but it didn't seem to matter. And once because I found the advice in a book, I boiled all my traps in a strong brew made from spruce twigs and bark. This was supposed to rid the traps of their metal odor and to protect them from rust. Maybe it did, but to the marten and lynx I trapped it seemed of no importance one way or the other.

Whatever was needed, the country always provided somehow—out of its soil and snow, and from those found tools, the dulling coils and edges men leave behind. I made lynx snares from strands of old windlass cable rescued from a dump on one of the mining creeks. Time in the late fall afternoons when the long grey light filled the porch windows, and I sat there unraveling cable, working with cutters and pliers, while my thoughts strayed outward to the river below the house and returned to the task at hand. Five or six strands were about right, twisted together and knotted at the ends in a figure eight. Sometimes I found it best to heat the wire over a flame to make it easier to work with or to change its color; the brightness burned to a dull metallic blue or grey, and was not so easily seen in the woods. When I had ten or a dozen snares made I wound them into small coils, tied them together, and hung the bundles from nails on the workshop beams. I had other snares that were factory made, with fancy metal locks, but I found them to be too long for most uses and wasteful of wire. I cut them down, making two out of one. Great numbers of snares were needed, for many would fail and be lost in the woods.

I went on foot, packing my gear for the day, or I went with the dogs overnight and for longer. The dogs went with a yelping rush when they could, or until they were winded, and there were times I preferred to trudge along at my own pace, to stop and spend some time in a new terrain. Or I might take the dogs and sled for a few miles, tie them, and go on afoot or with snowshoes. The snow might be deep or shallow, the season warmer than usual, or colder than the year before with long spells of wind and drifted trails. The best winters were those in which snowfall was light, and the worst cold passed in a few days' time—"The finest kind of trapping winter," as one old Finn trapper liked to put it.

However I came to it, from hints in books, or from the remarks of old neighbors, I understood quite early that I should not trap the country too hard. There was once a common attitude, and I suppose it may still be found, that one could move into a country, trap it of everything on four legs, and then move on. But that would not do for me. Although my awareness of these things was still half formed, I seemed to have had it in me as an instinct to care for the country that I might live in it again. Most animals in an unsettled land are not trap shy. It is possible to catch every marten and mink in the country, and the same will be true for lynx. A country trapped too hard, as my own Redmond creeks and hills had once been, may take a long time to recover, and a man living there will face lean years of his own making. As I watched the woods and listened to the talk of old trappers, I saw that it was best to leave a little seed in the country, and to trap according to the scarcity and abundance of the fur sign. It was all too uncertain at best; too many things intervene to make any cropping of the wild a secure and reliable thing, as if life had no purpose beyond our own uses for it. That year of great abundance may return, and the woods flourish; but the rabbits will leave us again some day, and nothing we can think of to do will bring them back until they are ready.

The trapping year turned on the winter solstice, a twilight world of lasting shadows and soft grey light. A cold sun clearing the mountains far to the south, the daylight hardly begun when it ended. I became a creature of the dusk, to be out early and home late, to begin in the dark and end in the dark. A trudging and packing, watching, and marking off the days. December went by, January and February. Perceptibly the days grew longer and the light stayed, though the cold often remained, deepening at night-fall. Marten season closed, beaver season opened and ran until April. A quickening came to the woods, felt in the long light and the sudden day of warmth. My mind began its return from snow and darkness to sunlight once more, to seeds and pots of earth.

And then with the onset of thaw in late spring, it was over. The traps were pulled, hung up, or stored away, the snares gathered in from the woods. I made my last trip with the sled and dogs over a softening trail, and put away harness and sled for the summer. The furs were counted and admired, the money already spent in mind. Some new things learned, some disappointments. Decisions for next year: a new trail needed to a farther creek, and a cache to be built there. One of the dogs has been acting up. So, as the sun gains power, and water drips from the cabin eaves, another year.

As I write this now, many things come to mind, half-buried under the stored-up debris of the years: scraps from books, words of advice, murmurs, glimpses into forgotten days and habits. I want to make a great list of them, as if in a moment they would pass from my mind forever.

The catalogue is endless. I begin with water sets and trail sets, with blind sets and cubby sets, with drowning stones and balance poles. The vocabulary clinks with chains and rasps with nooses. The exercise of an ancient cunning, schooled in the forest so far back that its origin is forgotten, the ruses handed down by voice and page, or rediscovered by the hand and eye in practice. So innocent a device as a "stepping stick," a length of dry willow, casually dropped across the trail, to lie there much as nature might have felled it; the trap set just beyond it and to one side, so that the forefoot of the animal comes squarely down as it walks or lopes along.

I hear these words from a dead man's journal: "I will first describe the most successful set I know of. . . ." A dead log spans a gully; it is so old that the bark has slipped and fallen, and the branches rotted away. But halfway across there is one dry stub standing crookedly in the air. And from it a round noose is suspended, propped above the log to bar the way. Something will cross there, who knows what; but come snowfall and a moonless night, we may find the creature hanging.

"A rabbit's head hung in a hollow tree. . . ." My list tells of baits and how to use them, of spoiled fish and rotted guts. How once on someone's advice I dragged a ripe chunk of moose paunch behind me for a couple of miles, setting traps as I went. It worked, too. Every marten that crossed my trail turned and followed it. I saw that foxes and coyotes liked to dig through the snow on the river bars for a dead salmon stranded in the fall. So I buried a piece of fish in the snow where I saw old tracks, and set my trap above it; I covered it all with snow and hoped for a little wind.

"This scent is made as follows: take equal parts of rabbit, skunk and muskrat, with two mice added, chop fine, place in a covered jar and allow to stand in the sun. . . ." And so the baits are refined into lures and scents, to the pungency of beaver castor chopped and ground, the reek of soured meats, of urine saved and droppings preserved. Rich and disturbing, the whole obscene and fascinating craft and science of it, set down, stored away in mind, to be searched out one day when its use is needed.

So many intricate methods of death, brooded upon and perfected. Once in an old book I found a chapter called "The Art of Pulling Hearts." It told how to kill small animals by reaching with a deft hand under the rib cage where the heart jumped and pounded—and with a sure pull downward the heartstrings snapped.

I became reasonably skilled at what I did, almost as if I'd been born to it, and this sometimes gave me trouble. I could not avoid thinking of the animals I caught, and of my own motives and craft. I lay awake at night, watching my trail in the snow overhead, and saw myself caught in a trap or snare, slowly freezing to death. I felt the cold grip of the metal, the frost in my bones. A pair of great yellow eyes seemed to stare at me from the darkness, and looked into my soul. Very likely I bestowed on the creatures more capacity for pain and suffering than they possess, but there was no way to be sure of this. Their lives and deaths haunted me like a wound in my own flesh.

Especially painful things would sometimes happen. Once on the river I caught a neighbor's dog in a coyote snare. He was long dead when I found him, the wire drawn up so tightly around his neck that his head was nearly severed from his body. The snow and torn brush gave evidence of a terrible struggle. I removed the snare from his neck with difficulty, and dragged the frozen body onto the midchannel ice to let the river have him. I told myself that it was not my fault; the neighbor, who lived several miles away, was careless and let his dogs run loose in the country. They often ran in a pack, and were a menace to young moose. Nevertheless, my regret over it was so keen that I set no more snares on the river close to home.

It was partly because of this persistent identification that I did not often attempt to trap beaver, though they were fairly common on the river sloughs. I disliked the idea of it to begin with, they were such hardworking animals, the engineers of the woods and waters, and too often pitted against careless men with their traps and guns, their roads and culverts. But at the same time, beaver were one of the few furs consistently worth money on the market, and three or four good pelts in those days would buy a lot of beans and bacon.

I caught my first beaver late one spring in a small pond on lower Tenderfoot. I put in a lot of time for that beaver, walking the six miles both ways from Richardson in a cold wind. I had little experience in it, and knew mostly what I had read and had been told by other trappers. And what it amounted to was work.

Snow covered the pond ice, and the beaver house was a large, irregular mound in the still-wintry landscape. I had a two-inch chisel mounted on a heavy six-foot pole. With this and a small shovel to clear the ice chips as I worked, I cut a hole two or three feet down in the ice. The brown pond water, released from its ice prison, surged up, foaming and bubbling, filling the hole to its brim. Sometimes the water kept on coming, staining the snow and flooding the ice around me. When that happened, I retreated to the shoreline where I cut some brush and poles to stand on while I continued to work with my chisel, making the hole large enough to take my trap.

I used the standard #4 beaver trap and baited it with a fresh piece of aspen. Other baits might be used—cottonwood was best, but willow would do, and aspen was handy close to the pond. From spruce poles cut near the pond I built a rough sort of tripod, nailed and wired together. The trap was set at the bottom of this, the bait stick nailed above it and blazed with the axe so that the white wood showed through the green bark to attract a beaver in the murky water. The entire contraption was let down into the water until the lower half of it, with trap and bait, was below the ice and resting on the bottom of the pond. The water in the open hole soon froze in the subzero air, and the set was fixed like concrete until I came next time to chop it loose.

All this had to be done with care, and at the right distance from the shoreline and the beaver house, or the work would go for nothing. After cutting a hole and testing the depth with a stick, I occasionally found that the water was too shallow. There was nothing for it then but to move farther out on the ice and try again. A twig standing up from the pond bottom, or a troublesome growth of weeds, might set off the trap before a beaver found it. Beaver were scarce on the ponds, and to me in my inexperience they seemed to be exceptionally wise. Twice I pulled up a trap to find it sprung and the bait stick gone.

But I came one bright morning to find my beaver at last. It came out of the water at the end of the trap chain, drowned and dripping. I looked at it there on the sunlit ice with mingled triumph and regret. It was big and dark, and must have weighed nearly forty pounds. It made a wet and heavy load in the basket going home to Richardson over the hill.

Sometime later I tried to catch beaver in the Tanana. I had chosen a new beaver house built on the bank of a slough below the mouth of Banner Creek, and marked it with a stick in the fall so that I could find it again in the spring. The Tanana overflowed many times that winter; a tremendous, multilayered sheet of ice built up on the slough, spilling over the shoreline, so that it seemed nothing could be alive beneath it. The beaver house itself was out of sight under the ice and impacted snow. But beaver season came, and I was going to try it.

Not far from where I thought the house was, and in what I thought would be the deepest part of the channel, I cut my way with the big chisel through six feet of ice before I struck water. Ah! I thought, as I stood there perspiring in the cold, while the ice-clear river water bubbled up in the hole—That should do it! But when I searched the depth with a long pole to see how much room I had, I found that I had reached only a two-foot pocket of water trapped in the ice, and there was more ice beneath. I gave it up, disgusted. The beaver in that house must have starved that winter, frozen in, unable to reach their food. Unlucky beaver.

It was hard work and low wages. Some of the old people used to say that there were few things more demanding. To stand out there in that amazing frost and handle the burning iron, often with thin gloves, or nothing at all on your hands, if the work must be done with care. Cold hands and cold feet, numbed and aching fingers. Nothing to eat all day but a frozen doughnut, or a piece of dried meat and a handful of snow. As Fred Campbell would sometimes say of himself as he danced up and down beside his trail on a cold morning, trying to stay warm, "whining like a pup" for the frost— "It was *that* cold!"

And it was not the cold alone, though that could be brutal enough. Traveling on the river ice and in the creek bottoms, there was always danger of stepping into overflow water and getting wet to the skin. Many a Far North trapper could tell of breaking through thin ice and plunging into knee-deep water, of the race to shore to build a fire, to warm and dry himself. If you got anything frozen out there, far from home and shelter, it was just too bad.

I have an image of myself bent over on the ice in Tenderfoot, my nose feeling as if it was about to split open in the minus-forty-degree frost; cursing, muttering to myself, as I tried with thick mitts or dead fingers to get that damned trap set just right. And come back days or weeks later to find no animal caught, but wind and snow over the set, the bait gone, the trap sprung, and nothing there at all for the time and work.

There were quiet days at home, in camp, skinning marten. The small carcass thawed overnight in a cool part of the cabin. In the morning I began with a knife, working down from the tail and back legs, pulling the skin from the cold, still-partly frozen body. A small-bladed knife was best around the toes and head. When the nose and lips came free, I stretched the wet skin inside out on a narrow board made for that purpose, and tacked it there, a thin splint holding the tail down flat.

I dried the skins carefully away from the heat, turning them on the boards, making the best of the work. And then with a few of my best furs I caught a ride to Fairbanks one morning—a long, cold ride in the back of someone's pickup, maybe. I made the rounds of the fur buyers in town, finally taking a price, never enough, but something, enough to buy the few things we needed.

With a sack of groceries I caught a ride home through the dark on the long, empty highway.

If success in the woods can be put into numbers, or measured at all with its many hidden rewards, my own was never great, but varied according to the fur supply and the time I was willing to give to trapping. In one good winter I have record of, I caught twenty marten, a couple of lynx, and one or two foxes. I was paid less than $300 for these when I sold them. That was a lot of money to us then, two-thirds of the year's income. And as I say that, I realize again how little we needed to live on in those years, and how important that little could be.

Not long ago, while stopped in a small settlement in Yukon Territory, I saw a local notice of fur prices for the coming fall. As I glanced over the list, I was astonished. $350 for a prime lynx! $250 for a red fox. Coyote to $150. And so on down to the always reliable marten, mink, and beaver. I thought back to my own days with envy. We were lucky to get $30 for a lynx, and the average was $15. You could hardly give away a fox skin, and except for the occasional bounty money, coyote were better left in the woods. As I turned away from the price list, I felt as if I'd spent a good part of my life in a bleak and impoverished age.

But as necessary as it seemed to be, and as welcome as the money was, I never really liked selling my furs. They were more to me than money—the satisfaction of a good job done, and the clean fur shining in the light. I felt the pride had gone into my pocket when they were sold.

I think of myself during those years as a passionate amateur, an intense and respectful intruder on an ancient domain. My trails and cabins were real, the dogs and much else, and I lived much of the time as if no other life or work could ever matter. But trapping was not for me the single, lifelong occupation it has been for others. I would yield to them the greater claim—masters and serious men in their own right, as many of them have been. But what I did had its own seriousness, and I learned from it what I wanted.

Another lifetime, perhaps, I might have remained and let the wilderness take me.

When some of the adventure of it had worn off, and we had another source of income, I did not trap again. But it was always there, a thing I could do if I had to, though my dogs were gone, sleds and harness sold, and fur prices lower than ever.

If I consider it now, with many details forgotten, prices and much else put aside, what I return to is the deep wonder of it. How it was to go out in the great cold of a January morning, reading the snow, searching in the strongly slanted shadows for what I wanted to see. And there were books to be read there, life histories followed sometimes to their end: a bit of fur matted in the stained ice, the imprint of an owl's wing in the snow.

A strange, mixed enjoyment. The smell of something victorious, to have worked that hard in the cold, and gotten something for my labor. To have outwitted that creature, set the trap or snare, and caught it. To discover by morning light something that lived and moved by night, and of which I had known nothing before but a foot pad left in the snow.

There might come that morning after a storm when I went with snowshoes to break out a trail in the deep drifts and wind; all the tree limbs bent over with snow, and no trail to be seen, the traps buried out of sight. It was far, far back in time, that twilight country where men sometimes lose their way, become as trees confused in the shapes of snow. But I was at home there, my mind bent away from humanity, to learn to think a little like that thing I was hunting. I entered for a time the old life of the forest, became part fur myself

Sometime there may come to us in a depleted world, the old hunter's dream of plenty. The rich country, full of game, fish, and fur, bountiful as it once was. The bear, the moose, and the caribou. The woods are thick with rabbits; the marten crossing and recrossing, their paired tracks always going somewhere in the snow under the dark spruces. And carefully, one foot before the other, the round, walking track of the lynx: they never seem to hurry. Beaver in the ponds, a goshawk beating the late-winter thickets like a harrying ghost; and now and then the vague menace of a wolf passing through.

This, or its sometime shadow: the country dead, and nothing to see in the snow. Famine, and the great dream passing.

Stories We Listened To

I T IS EVENING IN THE KITCHEN of the roadhouse at Richardson, past dusk of a winter day. A gas lantern is burning overhead, throwing strong light on the white enamel of the shelves and cupboards, a brightness on the hanging pots and pans. A white oilcloth marked with a well-rubbed floral pattern gleams on the long table in the center of the room.

Three of us are sitting at the table—Allison, Melvin, and myself—drinking coffee laced with strong rum. A heated and windy sigh comes from the flue of the Great Majestic range standing black and heavy at one end of the room.

Allison is speaking, relaxed at the end of a day of roadhouse chores. His favorite black chauffeur's cap is pushed back on a ruddy expanse of forehead; a worn pair of sheepskin mittens lies on the table by his left hand. Allison, who loves to tell a story, one ice blue eye fixed on his audience, telling of the things he has known and heard from the others.

"But you know, Bill . . ." He is speaking to Melvin . . . "And Haines, here—we mustn't forget him, you know. There's been some pretty strange things happened up here in our day—fellas too long out there on the trapline by themselves, and some of them a little funny in the head to begin with, if you know what I mean."

And Melvin is nodding in agreement, a little wary of Allison's stories, but willing enough to listen. He himself has lived over forty years at Richardson, and at seventy-eight is its oldest resident. His white hair is cropped above a strong, angular face, and upon his compact, wool-trousered frame he carries the alertness of a confident age. And he is saying in a quiet voice and with a level gaze directed to Allison that, yes, he knew of this or that person and event.

Then Allison, stirring his coffee with a heavy spoon, begins a story about two trappers who met and did not speak.

Solitary men in remote watersheds, each of them with a cabin and a team of dogs. And the winter wears on, the days briefer and darker, and then perceptibly a little longer and brighter. Circles are drawn around the calendar dates, and the leaves turned one by one. Silence, too much of it sometimes: the sound of frost cracking in the walls of the cabin, a wind in the spruce boughs overhead; the dogs barking at feeding time or howling at some distant wild voice. The same thoughts in the evenings, having come in from the cold and the long day out; the same pages read from the same catalogues and magazines; the same words muttered in some argument with the shadows. The same fat and cornmeal cooked in the big pot for the dogs at the same time each night; sleep, and the same light growing pale in the window late in the morning.

At last he must see someone, he feels. Not to talk, that would be too much; but just to see someone, to be with another person for a while. He knows of another trapper a long day's travel away on another creek. What is his name? It doesn't matter, he has to go. The sled is packed and the dogs harnessed. The morning is mild, and off he goes, breaking a new trail through the snow to his distant neighbor.

It was already dusk when he drove in sight of a low-roofed, roughly built cabin in spruce timber on a bench above a swampy creek. Someone was home, for smoke stood white and still above the short pipe in the snow roof. The dogs chained in the yard set up a din of barking at the strange team come so suddenly out of the trees.

He stopped his sled a little ways off at the edge of the woods with a grunted command to his dogs. As he unhitched and anchored his team for the night, the cabin door opened and another man stood framed in the doorway, looking at him across the cleared space of yard. He neither waved nor spoke, but turned back into the cabin, leaving the door ajar.

The man who had just arrived threw each of his dogs a chunk of frozen, half-dried fish from a bale on his sled. He took up his bedroll and walked through the yard, making his way among the five big dogs chained to their shelters, and who strained toward him, barking at his strangeness. When he reached the door of the cabin under the gable end of the roof he paused and looked back across the yard into the dusk. Then, stooping under the low door frame, he stepped inside and closed the door behind him.

He found the other man seated on a bench at the single table in the light of a lantern just lit: a man much like himself, a little older, maybe, with a greying stubble on his face, and with a thoughtful and piercing gaze.

The man who had just come into the cabin set his bedding on the floor. He took off his parka, shook it to remove the frost, and hung it from a spike near the door. He placed his mittens and his cap to dry on a rack above the dented, sheet-iron stove, and turned toward the table. He did these things slowly and deliberately as if unsure of his welcome. But the man who lived there nodded at him and motioned with his hand toward a small wooden keg upturned at the other end of the table.

The man who came sat down. He did not look again at his companion. He studied his hands for a moment and rubbed them, easing the stiffness from his finger joints. He glanced around at the interior of the small cabin, observing the familiarity of it, a place much like the one he had left that morning: a squared room built of peeled logs and with a smoke-darkened roof of poles; a window set in one wall, a space of rough plank floor between stove and table strewn with wood chips and stray fingers of straw.

The other man rose from his bench. He found two scarred enameled metal plates in a box on a shelf behind the stove, bent forks and spoons, and laid them out on the table. He returned to the stove where a black pot bubbled with meat and beans. And the two men sat and spooned out the steaming stew to their plates, and ate in silence.

The evening passes. The two men sit quietly, drinking tea. One of them dozes from fatigue and the warmth of the cabin, and wakes again with a start. The other rises now and then to put more wood on the fire, to clear the table and fill the kettle with water, after which he returns to his bench. The fire cracks, the lantern snores monotonously, and the evening wears on in silence.

After a time, the man on the bench rises, attends to the fire once more, and prepares for bed, just as he does each night at this time. The other man stands and unrolls his bedding on the floor in the space between stove and table. Each man unties his moccasins and hangs them from a nail in one of the roof beams. Long socks, heavy shirts and trousers are removed, the two men standing with their backs half-turned to each other, as if shy of the sudden company. Undressed to grey underwear, the two men lie down. The mantle in the lantern slowly flares to an amber glow, and the light goes out with a soft pop. Someone sighs deeply and turns in his bedding. A figure of darkness sits in the cabin, looking out at starlight on the snow.

There will be years of this life, he thinks; of the slow dawns and their light on the snow; years of this country, of its solitude and quiet. Or it will change, become crowded with sounds and new people, and he will not understand. He himself will grow old, grey, and stiff, bent to the cordwood and the trap. But for as long as he can walk or stand he will stay with this life of snow, of fur, of solitude and dogs.

Now something rises into his consciousness, something of his past, of the place he came from. Faces without names appear and fade, and there are one or two with names. Questions are put to him from the darkness into which he is sinking: voices, but they have grown strange to him. There is something that he knows and cannot put into words. He could never say to them, the shadows whose forms now fill his darkening mind, why he came here, chose this life without company, without solace of children or ease for his age. He hardly remembers the reasons, the long-ago decisions. There was the finality of leaving, of saying good-bye; a landscape he would not see again, a people he would never hear from. All that has become part of an immense distance, part of a sleeping self.

Morning came early, much earlier than the slow grey light at the single window. It came as a gradual chill to the cabin, as a muffled chain-rattle in the yard where a dog emerged from its shelter to stretch and shake itself.

The man sleeping on the bunk yawned and threw back his blankets. He sat up briefly in the dim light before striking a match and lighting the candle wedged in the end of an empty tin on a box beside the bunk. He rose to his feet in the yellow, flickering light and, avoiding with care the prone figure on the floor, with torn strips of birch bark and fine dry kindling he fired the stove, then filled the kettle with water from a bucket.

As the fire drew and crackled, the other man moved in his blankets and sat up. He saw the shadowy configuration of the room around him, was aware of the presence of another man, and knew he was not in his own place. As the small room warmed, he dressed himself and rolled up his bedding, while his silent companion moved with care between the stove and the table.

Soon there was coffee, oatmeal with raisins, and sourdough bread in a pan. And neither man said a word to the other, each one absorbed in his thoughts. From long habit, each of them knew the right thing to do at that hour: a glance out the door at the morning sky, another look with the candle at the thermometer on the wall outside the window. An armful of wood for the stove, a bucket of snow for water. And each returned to his bench or his keg, to sit once more looking into some deep shadow in the room.

It was full daylight now, as full as the brief winter day would allow: a rose-grey light beyond the hills to the south, a transparent twilight on the snow. It was time for him to leave.

The man who came tugged the laces of his moccasins and tied them. He stood up and took his mittens from the rack, his parka from the wall, his bedding from the floor. He paused, as if now finally he would speak, half-turned to the man still sitting beside the table. Then he opened the door and stepped out into the yard.

His moccasins made a dry, crunching sound on the packed snow as he walked to the edge of the woods where his dogs were standing, roused and shaking themselves, beginning to whine. He broke his sled loose from the snow and packed it once more. His movements were quick and sure now. He laid the cold, stiff harness out on the snow, and one by one he snapped his dogs into the towline.

The other man came to the door of the cabin. He stood watching as the man at the edge of the yard spoke something quietly to his dogs, and they moved off swiftly onto the broken trail, heading home.

Allison pours a little rum into his cup and shoves the bottle across the table. I see the familiar red and yellow label: *Lemon Hart, Demarara Rum, 151 Proof.* Melvin is watching in his guarded and knowing way; he will have no more rum, at his age he doesn't drink much. I cannot tell if he believes the story, but he smiles a little crookedly and looks at me from under shaggy eyebrows as if he would share with me some comment that he cannot speak aloud.

I have said little, sitting across the table from Allison. I am silent because I am young, and because I have almost nothing to tell; it is my place to listen now, watching the faces and gestures of these two men long past their youth.

The talk goes on: questions, assertions, a careful sparring among things remembered, called up on impulse from years shared in a country whose thinly settled people have been like members of a restless family. And as I listen, something fills the pauses and surges in their talk, as in some interval of quiet comes now and then a sigh from the great range by the kitchen wall. I find myself for a time included in a vanished company—of men camped or on the move, hunting, tree-falling, digging, sometimes together and often apart. Their voices rise and fade: guttural exclamations, curses, and impatient whispers. From Kansas, Ontario, Michigan—yoked to the single, confused prospect. . . . With chain and whip, by wagon and sledge, by boat and rail, and by foot; over soaked sod and dry snow, drawn forward with creaking axles and squealing runners. They pass, knotted and dispersed, in a solitude without women.

Who comes here, to this whiteness, this far and frozen place, in search of something he cannot name? Not wealth, it may be, but a fortune of the spirit, a freshness denied him in the place he came from. The North glitters and brightens; the land grows dark again, and the fugitive glow from a gas mantle lights the shadows.

Allison fills the cups with coffee, pouring out of a big blue granite pot brought from the stove. He stands beside the table in a half-buttoned, dark brown sweater—a short man in his late sixties, erect and broad in the chest. Now he takes the lantern down from its hook in the ceiling. He closes a thumb over the end of the pump rod and works it. The mantles brighten, and the sound of the forced and burning air grows loud again.

Now Melvin remembers something about a bear. I imagine he knows as much about bears and about the woods as any man I have met; certainly he has forgotten more than I will ever know. And quietly, as of something chosen at ease from a great storehouse, he begins to tell how once, long years ago, he traveled through the Stewart River country with a party of men on foot.

It was getting on toward the middle of fall, and they were on their way back to Dawson from a recent stampede, eager to record their staked parcels of ground and return to the creeks before winter caught them. Late one afternoon they caught up with a big grizzly who was walking the trail before them. With the bear in sight ahead, the party halted.

They were in a narrow canyon of the river, on a trail recently cleared by a telegraph crew. The river lay sheerly below them on one side, and a steep rock face pitched above them on the other. There was no way around that bear, and strangely in that party of stampeders, no one had brought a gun.

The bear himself was in no hurry, rolling fat and densely haired, heading into winter. The hump on his black shoulders rippled as he moved along. Becoming aware of the men behind him, he turned and rose to his full height, peering toward them where they were gathered in a group sixty yards away. Then, satisfied they were no threat to him, the bear dropped back to all fours and went leisurely on his way.

The men camped at nightfall as well as they could on the narrow shelf of the trail, making a scanty fire from the few dry sticks and tough green shrubs they found on the slopes around them. They hoped the bear would be gone next day. Winter was coming, a little snow in the air at times; food was low, and none of them knew the country well; they were anxious to be in town.

But soon after breaking camp in the morning, as they picked their way on the rough trail with their heavy packs, they caught up with the bear again. And there they waited. It was his country and his season, and he was not going to be pushed. Impatient, but with no other choice, they traveled the day at the bear's deliberate pace.

For three days the party was forced to walk behind that bear. It was a slow and exasperating journey, the bear taking time to dig for roots along the trail, upending rocks in search of mice. Or he would stop at any time of the day to sleep, sprawled out in the middle of the trail like a great rug-heap, stretching his long-nailed, hairy toes and snapping his jaws in the air, while the men watched from a distance.

One or two of the men, more foolish than the rest, got angry. They shouted at the bear and threw rocks toward him. Unused to any animals but dogs and horses, the bear to them was only a big nuisance, an unruly pet, a zoo creature out of place in the landscape. They were lucky in their ignorance, for the bear only turned and growled at them if they came too close.

Then, late in the third day, as they approached a wooded break in the canyon, the bear, who was now only a short distance ahead of them, stopped again. He turned, rose once more to a thick and imposing presence, and looked steadily at the men gathered behind him. They could see plainly the thick dark fur of him, slightly ruffled by a breeze, shining in the thin fall sunlight that came from across the river through a gap in the canyon wall. The big, round face of the bear regarded them, his blunt nose searching the air. It was the assured and measuring look of the undisputed master of things.

Finally and, as it seemed, with great dignity, the bear dropped down again and turned away. As if he had known all along exactly where he was going, he climbed easily among some tumbled boulders, and with a muffled cracking of dry brush he vanished uphill in the scattered timber.

Melvin is quiet again. He has none of Allison's flair for drama, but speaks matter-of-factly, and never insists on an audience. Another time, when he and I are alone in his cabin by the river, he will talk, the faraway things he remembers coming almost casually if he thinks I want to hear.

We drink, coffee or rum, and a few more words are spoken on the subject of bears. There are names and incidents: Fred Campbell, for instance, and his loose-running pack of dogs, chasing every bear in the country to keep the dogs fed. A damned nuisance, Melvin says; no one could find a moose because of the commotion he raised.

I learn of bears in the Democrat cookhouse, rattling the pots and dishes, pulling down shelves and boxes, while the men listening from the next room through the log wall plotted how to chase them out. Of a bear named Teddie that Melvin raised from a cub, keeping him tamed with a stout stick, until in its fourth year the bear became surly and aggressive and had to be shot.

A chronicle of the wise, the foolish, and the lucky—it will be resumed one evening when we are here again, to renew the playful innocence of an early day when men could stand in wonder at a beast, to marvel at a world abundant with things that walked and flew and swam and seemed possessed of understanding, to speak at times almost like men themselves.

From somewhere back in my own memory now I pull together a few phrases from a far more recent spring. They tell in the plain prose of a daily newspaper how a well-known big-game guide and his wealthy hunter, missing for over a week in the Alaska Range, had been found dead, killed by the grizzly they had tried to smoke from his den. It was front-page Interior news at the time, one of those stories that stamp the season with the unmistakable aura of tragedy or adventure. And I remember so well how old Delmar Elliot, a long-gone neighbor, talked about it as we drove along one morning on the road into Fairbanks. He related the story as he had heard it, from start to finish, methodically, in detail, as if he wanted the story told right for some page of local history, and concluding in his flat-toned, serious way: "The bear bit 'em . . . I guess that's why they died."

But it is deep winter now, and all the bears are sleeping. There are other things to think of—keeping warm, for instance. Allison, turning the bottle of rum in a broad hand, mentions a name: Jim Chisholm, who owned a cabin on Birch Lake back in the thirties. A drinking man, single, past middle age, careless with stove and fire.

And one cold night in December, when he had stoked the fire too hot and gone to bed, sparks from a bad pipe-joint caught in the dry roof-moss above the stove. Chisholm was roused from heavy sleep by the heat and smoke of a fire burning at one end of the cabin—hot flames eating the dry poles as if they were paper. Confused, clad only in a thin nightshirt, he had time and thought to grab a robe and thrust his feet into a pair of slippers before he ran through the blazing doorway to the snow outside.

It was thirty below and thinly overcast, one of those nights when you must look a long time to see the far shore of a lake.

Chisholm stood in the glare-lit darkness in slippers and loose robe, half-warmed by his blazing cabin, as log after log caught, and then a part of the roof came down in a shower of sparks.

Two miles distant across the snow and ice of the lake were his nearest neighbors in a lodge on the Valdez road. With nothing left to him in the fire and settling ashes, he turned toward the ice-bound lake and began to walk.

It was a long walk in daylight on a firm trail. Chisholm plowed along, missing the trail, stumbling in the dry, lightly drifted snow that came at times to his knees. He was urged on by a growing fear, as he held his arms crossed on his chest, clutching the robe to his body, its narrow collar partly wrapped about his face and ears. He no longer felt the cold snow in his slippers, but sensed instead a pricking numbness growing upward into his legs. He was fully awake and breathing hard, staring into the snow, into the wind that came now and then across the frozen lake, toward what he thought he could see half-lighted in the timber on the far shore.

In the kitchen of the small roadhouse at the south end of the lake, two men whose names are not recorded were drinking late coffee and washing up for the night. There was little traffic in the winter, sixty miles out from Fairbanks, and at that late hour no travelers were expected. But after a while in the stillness they heard a sound outside, a slow and measured thumping on the steps that rose to the porch.

Here, Allison, in a dramatic gesture, lifted the bottle of rum and brought it down on the table ... bump ... bump ... bump. ... That was the sound they heard.

One of the men went to the door with a lantern and opened it to the night. And there in the still cold was Chisholm, coming slowly across the snow-cleared boards. His robe clung loosely about him, he had long since lost his slippers. He lifted each leg as if it was made of wood, and let the bare, hard foot fall with a heavy thump. And then he stopped and stood in the light of the lantern, peering out from the frost that clung to his hair and the collar of his robe, unable to lift his head or unclasp his arms, unable to speak for the great cold that was in him.

The two men, roused into action, brought him into the warmth of the kitchen and sat him down in a chair before the stove. They did this gently, with care not to bruise or break his frozen flesh. A blanket was warmed and wrapped about him. Hot coffee was poured and brought to him, the cup tilted to his lips, a little at a time, until he could speak and could tell what had happened.

His feet and lower legs were like dead things, nearly hard and white as marble. It looked bad, but something had to be done. A five-gallon tin of coal oil was standing in the kitchen, warm from the heat of the room. A washtub was brought in from the pantry and set on the floor by the stove. Chisholm's feet were placed within it, and the coal oil was carefully poured into the tub. One man knelt on the floor by the tub and began to massage his legs with the warm oil, lifting it with his hands, rubbing down from the stiff knees, letting the skin and numbed flesh soften as he worked.

An hour passed, and something more than an hour, as the men traded places on the floor beside the tub. As they worked, and the surrounding warmth took effect, color gradually came back to Chisholm's face and body; very slowly sensation returned to his legs and feet, and with it a terrible pain.

"Well, you know," said Allison, leaning toward us and gripping the rum bottle in his hand, "it took both of those fellas to hold him down in the chair when the feeling came back in his feet. He yelled and moaned and fought like hell, but they saved him. I tell you, old Chisholm was pretty damned lucky. He may have lost a couple toes, but he walked on those feet and legs till the day he died."

The bottle of rum stands on the table before us, the dark liquor a few fingers down in the brown glass. Allison stares at us across the gleaming oilcloth with his one good eye, having spoken with a kind of finality, the slim note of affirmation still on his lips. So ends that story, as true as any you'll hear.

It is late, nearly midnight. Allison yawns and pushes his chair back from the table. He must bring in another bucket of coal and check the fire for the night. Melvin agrees it is time for him to be going. Time too for me to walk that mile and a half uphill to home.

We all get to our feet and reach for our mitts and parkas. Allison follows us out to the door, carrying the lantern and an empty scuttle.

Through the opened door a sudden rush of cold air comes in from the night. We stand a moment together on the porch to see the stars. Clear frost tonight, maybe ten below—not so bad. "Pretty good winter so far, by golly!"

"Good night, Bill. Good night, Haines. See you soon." Allison's words are followed by the sound of a shovel grating on the frozen, gravelly earth. A bulky figure bending in the lantern light by the coal shed, the nodding, deliberate movements of his arms and body are lengthened into shadows on the snow.

Melvin says good night in a clear voice; he walks across the road, a flashlight held before him, walking firmly toward his cabin, a quarter mile off by the river.

I begin walking the road in the other direction, toward Banner Creek, into the snow-lighted darkness. Under starlight, the snow glitters faintly. The shadowy, wooded crest of Richardson Hill rises before me. My moccasins crunch softly in the roadside snow. There is no other sound in the night. Nothing, not even the wind.

Out of the Shadows

I T WAS EARLY IN JULY. I was on my way to Cabin Creek, eight miles distant by trail in the Redmond drainage. I intended to make a quick overnight trip to secure our hunting cabin for the season and to see what the prospects might be for blueberries later that summer.

For company I had brought with me our youngest dog, a female husky named Moppet. She was nearly two years old, a quiet, alert, and intelligent animal. Glad to be along, to have been chosen, she trotted ahead of me on the trail, the thick grey and white plume of her tail swinging from side to side.

I was carrying my big pack basket containing a small axe, some food, and an old sweater to wear in the evening. I was also carrying one of the two rifles I owned, an ancient 8mm Mannlicher carbine I had inherited from an old resident in the country. It had once been a fighting weapon of the German Army in World War I. It had a scarred stock and a worn barrel, but was compact and light and easy to carry.

We had left home early to take advantage of the morning coolness. Now, five miles out, with the sun high at our backs on the open, sloping bench above Redmond Creek, the midmorning was clear and warm. As always here, the trail was wet underfoot, the moss and the dark sod still soaking from the spring runoff. Mosquitoes and small gnats rose out of the moss; a continual and shifting cloud of them swarmed about us.

As we walked along, skirting one dark pool of meltwater after another, I was thinking of many things: of the summer before me, of the fishing about to begin, the hoped-for success of the summer garden, and not too far ahead another hunting season. I took casual note of the places where in the winter just past I had set my traps: a shelter of twigs and sticks fallen together, and every so often under the lower boughs of a spruce tree standing near the trail a rusty marten trap was hanging, wired to its toggle stick.

It was a typical summer day in the subarctic backcountry. I was alone with a dog in a country that with its creeks, ridges, and divides, and with the high, brown slope of Banner Dome visible to the north, was as familiar to me as any suburban backyard. On the changing features of the landscape I seemed to see written my own signature of use.

We rounded the steep spruce-clad prow of the hill above Glacier Creek and stopped briefly at a cache I kept there below the point of hill. Here, three years before and late in the fall, we had camped in a tent while hunting moose. The ground poles of our tent were lying where we had left them under the trees. It was not hard for me to visualize things as they had been then: the grey slope of the canvas tent, smoke from the stovepipe, and snow in the wind. For a few weeks that tent had been home. Moppet was not yet born. Now I looked up at the narrow platform of the cache fixed solidly in the three spruces above me. A half-dozen traps were hanging from a spike in one of the supports. The ridgepole of the tent and the rest of its framework were pitched together and standing upright against the cache to keep them dry. I saw that everything was as I had left it when I stopped here with the dogs and sled on the last snow of the season.

We left the cache and went on down the trail toward the creek. The brush was thick, of dense, small-statured black spruce interspersed with thickets of alders. The trail wound about so that at no time could I see more than thirty feet ahead of me. Moppet was now out of sight somewhere ahead and probably waiting for me at the crossing.

As I came out of the woods and onto the open bench above the creek, I saw Moppet sitting at the edge of the steep slide down which the trail led to the creek bottom. Her ears were pricked sharply forward, and she was staring intently at something in the creek.

When I came up to her, I saw what she was watching. Down in the creek and less than twenty yards away, the shoulders and back of a large brown animal showed above the heavy summer grass and clumps of ice-cropped willows. It was moving slowly downstream at the far edge of an island that divided the creek.

At first I thought the animal was a young moose feeding on the fresh grass or on some waterplants in the shallow stream-course. And yet there was something about its size and bulk and the way that it was moving that was not quite familiar. And then the creature's head came into partial view, and I saw how the brown hump of its shoulders rippled as it moved. It was a bear, larger than any bear I had yet seen in that country. One look at that heavy square head and the shoulder hump, and I knew we had met a grizzly.

No more than a minute passed as I stood there with Moppet at my feet, watching the big bear in the grass below us. I was glad now that I had not brought one of our other dogs who would have immediately rushed barking into the creek after the bear. I was grateful for this quiet and obedient animal sitting at my feet with her hair stiffened on her shoulders and her nose twitching.

Where I stood at that moment I had an easy shot broadside into the bear's chest or shoulders. I could perhaps have killed it then and there. But I did not want to leave a dead bear to rot in the creek, and we were too far from home to pack out more than a small portion of the meat.

In the brief time that we stood there, I quickly went over my choices. We could not proceed down into the creek and follow the trail across to the opposite bank; the bear was by now directly in our path. We could stay where we were and let the bear go on downstream if that was its intention. But would Moppet remain quiet long enough?

I thought of easing away from the scene, of moving upstream

far enough to cross without disturbing the bear. It would have to be done quickly and quietly. At any moment the bear might discover us, or the noise of our retreat might alarm it. In an emergency there were no trees large enough to climb, and there was no hope of outrunning an aroused bear in that wet and spongy ground. My one advantage lay in the fact that we were above the bear and that it had not yet discovered us.

But the bear soon left me no choice. Something in our unseen presence on the bank above the creek, some sound, some prickling sense that it was not alone, seemed to change the bear's intentions. It stopped feeding. Its head came up, and it began to move more rapidly through the grass. As it did so, it turned in our direction. It was now in full view, no more than fifty feet away, and closing the distance between us.

In my sudden alarm that grizzly loomed larger and more of a threat than any black bear or bull moose I had ever met with. I was ready to fire, but in those swift moments I thought I might be able to frighten the bear, and by some noise or movement scare it back into the woods. Still holding my rifle, I raised my arms over my head. In what seems now to have been a ridiculous gesture, I waved my arms and did a small dance on the moss; I yelled and hooted and hoped. But the sudden noise, coming out of the stillness, seemed only to panic the animal. It broke into a loping run, heading directly toward us, and had already reached the bottom of the bank below us. I had no choice now. I put the rifle to my shoulder, took hurried aim at the heavy chest of hair below that big head, and fired.

At the sound of the gunshot the bear abruptly stopped a few feet below. It rose on its hind legs and stood at full height in front of us. In a rush of images I saw the stocky, upright length of its body, a patch of pale fur on its underthroat, the forepaws raised in a defensive gesture; I saw the blunt muzzle and the suddenly opened jaws. The bear growled loudly, swung its head to one side, and tried to bite at its chest. I was ready to fire again, and at that moment I might have put a shot squarely into its thick neck or broad upper chest. But for some reason in those tense seconds I again held my fire.

The bear dropped to the ground. It turned away from us and ran back through the grass and brush in a tremendous, lunging gallop, scattering leaves and splashing water. I watched it climb the bank on the opposite side of the creek and disappear. A heavy crashing came from the dry alders on the far side, and then all was still.

I stood at the top of the bank with my rifle half raised, listening. Over everything in that sudden stillness I was aware of my heart as a loud pounding above the calm trickle of water in the creek below. I heard a low whine, and glanced down. All this time Moppet had remained crouched and quiet at my feet. But now she rose with her hair bristling, searching the air with her nose, trying to catch some scent of that enormous creature so suddenly discovered and now vanished.

I moved away from the trail and walked a short distance upstream to where a bulky, crooked spruce grew at the edge of the bank. It was as large as any tree in the vicinity, and for some reason I felt more comfortable standing close to it. I removed my pack and set it on the ground beside me. I placed my rifle against the tree while I searched in my shirt pocket for tobacco and papers. In those days I was an occasional smoker. With trembling hands I rolled a cigarette, lit it, and smoked in silence.

It had all happened so quickly. Perhaps no more than three minutes had elapsed since I had first seen the bear. Now that I had some space in which to think, I realized that I had been extremely lucky. Had the bear not stopped, a second shot might have killed it, but if not, there would have been no way I could have escaped at least a severe mauling.

Somehow in that blur of excitement and indecision, I knew that I would not turn and run. Out of whatever stubborn sense of my own right to be there, or simply from an obscure pride, I would stand my ground, fire my shot, and from then on fend off the wounded bear as best I could, using my rifle for a club. In that event I would most likely have been killed, or I would have been so badly maimed that I could never have made it home without help, and there was no help anywhere near. Days might have passed before anyone came looking for me.

I stood there and smoked, gradually coming to some calm in myself. I could hear nothing from the woods on the far side of the creek. There was not the slightest movement to be seen in the brush growing upon that low bank, nothing at all in the grass below. From time to time I gazed up or down the creek as far as I could see above the willows and alders. Nothing.

I did not know how badly hit that bear was. Perhaps it was now lying dead over there. Or it might only be wounded, lying in the brush near the trail, gathering its strength and waiting for me to pass. At such times events and probabilities seem magnified; fear has a thousand faces.

I finished my cigarette, and picked up my pack and my rifle. I knew that I would have to go down into the creek and search the sand and grass for blood. Whatever I found, I would follow the bear's path across the creek and into the woods. I wanted above all to be on my way to the cabin and out of any further trouble. But first I had to be sure of that bear.

I waited another few minutes. Then, with Moppet at my heels, I returned to the trail, and we began our descent into the creek.

At the bottom of the bank I easily found the place where the bear had stood up after I fired at him. His big tracks were pressed deeply into the wet sand, the long toenails and the pad marks clearly outlined at the edge of the small channel.

Slowly and quietly I began to trace the bear's path through the grass. Stopping frequently to look around me over the grass and through the brush, I followed as well as I could the paw marks in the sand and the muddy sod. Where I could not see his tracks, I guided myself by the bent and broken grasses in the deep trough of the bear's passage. As I walked, half crouched, searching the ground, I examined with care every blade of grass and every leaf on the willows. But I found no sign of blood.

We went on through the grass and brush. Across the far channel we found the trail, climbed the shallow bank, and entered the woods. Moppet remained at my heels, at times pressing closely against my leg. Although I tried quietly to coax her, she would not go ahead but stayed close behind. The hair on her shoulders and neck was stiffened, and as she looked from side to side into the woods a muted and anxious throaty sound came from her, half growl and half whine.

Once up the bank and into the woods, we stopped. It was spooky as hell under that shadowy, sun-broken canopy of leaves. I searched the woods around me for the slightest movement and listened for any sound: a wounded breathing, a growl, anything. Nowhere in all that wilderness could I hear a sound above the muted purling of water in the creek behind me, and the song of a fox sparrow somewhere in the water-course.

We walked on, following the trail where it skirted the edge of a narrow ravine holding a wayward tributary of the creek. To cross the ravine I had built a rough bridge out of spruce poles. On the far side the trail turned upstream and continued through a swamp toward Cabin Creek.

When Moppet and I had crossed the bridge, I stopped again. Here an old game trail, deeply cut into the moss, intersected our sled trail and took its narrow, twisting way downstream. I hesitated. Nothing I had seen so far convinced me that the bear was at all wounded, but I was still not satisfied. I stepped into the game trail and began a careful circuit of the downstream woods into which I had seen the bear vanish. As quiet as it was, as eerily still, I felt that somewhere in that dim tangle of alders, willows, and dwarf birch the bear must be lying and listening to our movements. As in an episode of warfare, a pervasive uneasiness seemed to divide the shadows and the sunlight. I had that acute sense of being watched and listened to by an invisible foe. Each twig-snap and wave of a bough seemed a potential signal.

After about twenty minutes of what I considered to be a reasonably careful search, I returned to the trail. I now felt, from the lack of any blood sign or other evidence, that the bear had not been badly hit. I decided not to pursue the search any further. With Moppet following me, I went on through the swamp, climbing steadily toward the saddle that divided Glacier from Cabin Creek. We went carefully, every so often stopping to look back down the trail behind us. We were well away from the creek before Moppet would put aside her fear and go ahead of me.

It seemed to me now that I had merely grazed the underside of the bear's chest. I had fired downhill at a running target, and had aimed low. Moreover, the front sight of the old carbine had been damaged years ago and repaired with solder in a makeshift fashion. The gun sight was uncertain at best.

So obviously I had fired too low, and the bear had suffered no more than a nasty sting from the heavy 230-grain bullet I was using. Had the bear been solidly hit, there would surely have been blood somewhere, and there would by now be a dead or dying bear in the woods. As we came down off the hill on the last half-mile stretch to the cabin I began to feel a great deal easier, satisfied that I had not left a badly wounded animal behind me, and glad too that we had gotten off from the encounter ourselves with no more trouble.

We spent the night at the cabin. I fed Moppet and cut some firewood. In the late afternoon I did a few needed chores about the cabin. On going to the creek for a bucket of water, I found a few unripe blueberries among the bushes overhanging the deep, wet moss hummocks beside the creek. The berries were scattered, and it did not seem to me that they would be worth a trip later to pick them. As the evening light deepened over the hills and the air grew cooler, a thrush sent up its spiraling song from the aspens on the hillside across the creek. Mosquitoes whined at the screen door. Otherwise, things were very quiet there on the hill above Cabin Creek.

The following morning I secured the cabin for the remainder of the summer. I set a strong barricade over the door, and closed and nailed heavy shutters over the two windows. In the late morning Moppet and I set out for home.

As we came down through the swamp near Glacier, Moppet once more dropped behind me and refused to go ahead. I walked quietly with the rifle safety off and my hand half closed on the trigger. Again I watched the brush and listened to either side of the trail for the slightest sound. There was nothing but the quiet sunlit air of a summer day.

We crossed the creek, striding the small channels and pushing aside the grass, and on the far side we climbed the bank again. When we came to the top, I looked down. There, squarely in the trail and almost exactly where I had stood the day before when I fired at the bear, was a fresh mound of bear dropping. Nearby lay the spent shell from my rifle.

I looked closely at the dropping. It contained a few unripe blueberries, seeds, and other matter. It was still wet, though not warm. Moppet sniffed at it, and the grizzled hair once more rose on her neck and shoulders. For a moment my uneasiness returned, that vague, shivery sense of being watched and followed. The bear was still around, alive and well. Dangerous? I had no way of knowing.

The bear had probably not run far on the previous day, but had found a place in which to lie and lick its wound, baffled as to the source of its sudden hurt. It had heard us pass on the trail, had heard every sound of my passage in the brush, had followed every detail of my search. Perhaps much later in the evening it came out of its hiding place, out of the late cool shadows, and returned to the trail. It had stood where we were standing now, with its great, shaggy head down, sniffing the moss, the wet, black sod, trying to place in its dim sense of things an identity it would carry with it for the rest of its life.

I looked back down into the grass and brush of the creek from which we had just come. I turned and looked ahead of me to where the stubby black sprucewood closed in around the trail. If the bear was still somewhere in that dense green cover, nursing its hurt and its temper, waiting for revenge, it would have its chance.

But nothing vengeful and bloody came out of the woods to meet us as we went on up the trail. The walk home by Redmond, the long uphill climb to the homestead ridge passed without further incident. We came down off the hill as on many another occasion, to the sunlit vista of the river and the highway, to the sound of the dogs' furious barking. I had a good story to tell, and Moppet was petted and praised for her wise behavior.

In many subsequent hikes over the trail to Cabin Creek, in hunting forays along the benches above Glacier, we never saw that bear again. Now and then in late summer and early fall a blue mound of dropping in the trail gave evidence of a bear in the country, and that was all.

Never before or since have I been so rattled on meeting an animal in the woods. Years later, when I began to think of writing these pages, I rehearsed for myself another outcome to the adventure. I described in detail how the bear, badly hit in its lungs, had waited in the brush on the far side of the creek. When Moppet and I went by on the trail, the bear suddenly lunged from its hiding place with a terrible, bubbling roar and struck me down.

In that instant of confusion and shock I was joined to the hot blood and rank fur at last. All my boyhood dreams of life in the woods, of courage and adventure, had come to this final and terrifying intimacy.

Following the initial shock, as I lay sprawled by the trail with the bear standing hot and wounded above me, I managed to regain a grip on my rifle. Although stunned and, as it seemed, half-blinded, I raised the short muzzle of that ancient weapon and got off one last shot into the bear's throat. And with the sound of that shot in my ears, I lost consciousness.

In what may have been an hour or only minutes, I returned to a dazed sense of myself. I sat up, struggling to free myself of the things that seemed to hold me: my pack harness, torn clothing, and bits of broken brush. I seemed to look at myself and my surroundings from a great distance through a sun-dazzled semidarkness. I was still alive, though in the numbed, head-ringing silence I knew I was hurt, badly cut and bitten about my face and body. Moppet was gone. A short distance away from me the bear lay dead.

Somehow, maimed, stiffened, and bleeding, using a dry stick for a crutch, I found my way home. Patched and scarred, I wore my changed face as an emblem of combat, and walked in my damaged body to the end of my days, survivor of a meeting terrible and true.

Burning a Porcupine

I HAVE NEVER EATEN A PORCUPINE. The seasonal abundance of meat, fish, berries, and garden food made the taking of such animals unnecessary. But the dogs had to be fed by whatever means; between fish runs the pot was sometimes lean, and a small amount of fat meat went a long way.

In those rich Interior summers, when so many creature-things were awake, breeding and flourishing, it was not difficult to find a porcupine. Sometimes one would show up in the yard or the garden in the evening, shuffling through on its blind, mysterious travel. Often it was the dogs, turned loose for a run, who would find it. We heard a furious barking up the creek, and soon enough a dog came home with a dose of quills in its nose. Backtracking the woods, I found the mild, offending creature still holding its ground. A sharp blow on its blunt, black snout was sufficient to kill it: the stout, quill-bristled body slowly relaxing, a light in the dull, black eyes growing dim.

With the porcupine dead, came the preparation and use of the meat. The quills, those fiery-pointed arrows so lethal to dogs and other predators, had to be gotten rid of. There was a method, as there always is, a right way to do a thing. Years ago I learned how to burn a porcupine from Fred Campbell one late-summer day at his lake camp, far in the headwater hills behind Richardson.

We had caught the porky on our way back from McCoy Creek the previous evening. We heard Fred's dogs barking somewhere ahead of us on the trail, and knew they had found either a bear or a porcupine. Listening, I could not have said which it was, but Fred, from the shrill intensity of the din, guessed that it was a porky and that the dogs had it cornered.

There is the rare dog that in a given instance seems to know exactly what needs to be done. Campbell had such a dog, an ugly, scarred bitch named Judy, who with a sure sense of purpose, knowing that the creature would be killed and that the killing meant meat, always managed to corner the porky and keep it until he arrived.

We found the porcupine making a stand with its head lowered and its rear end armed with that powerful, quill-studded tail exposed to the excited dogs. One of the younger dogs had a few quills in its nose; wise Judy, standing well back and out of reach, barked and waited.

Fred killed the porcupine with his walking stick, a good solid blow on its head. He flipped it over and gutted it on the spot, dividing the liver with his knife and tossing a piece of it to each of his dogs. He placed the entrails high in a tree-crotch out of reach—the intestines were likely to be full of worms, and it was best not to let the dogs have any part of them raw.

We pulled the few quills from the one dog's nose, and packed up. Even with the guts removed, the dead weight of the porcupine made a heavy load in Fred's pack basket. We had had a long day, but we were close to camp and the meat was needed.

The following day Fred took the cooled body of the porcupine down from the roof of his cabin where he had cached it during the night. I was curious as to how he was going to remove the quills in order to feed the meat to the dogs. I ventured the observation that it would be a damned nuisance to skin it. Fred only grunted and told me to watch if I wanted to learn.

In the grassy yard in front of the cabin he scraped away a patch of sod to expose the sandy mineral soil underneath. He gathered up some dry sticks of wood, and with a strip of birch bark he built a small fire. As soon as the flames were leaping out of the brushwood, he placed the carcass of the porcupine on the fire. Immediately a plume of white and yellow smoke rose, and with it the sour, pungent smell of burning hair.

Fred adjusted the carcass on the fire, lifting it now and then to prevent it from smothering the flames. As the quills were singed, he took a short stick and beat the burned section clean, then turned the porky on the fire to expose another patch of hair and quills to the flames. Where the heat was intense, fat bubbled from the hide and dripped on the flames that flared up in a sudden, intenser blaze.

Those of Fred's dogs that were loose paced around the shifting smoke-haze, waiting for a burned piece of meat to come their way; the others, chained to their houses, followed every detail with eyes that seemed to blaze up with every flare of the fire.

And so it went, the fire replenished if need be, the carcass turned and returned. The singeing and the beating with a stick continued until all the hair and quills were burned off, and the scorched and blackened body was bare.

With the quills gone, Fred laid the carcass on a wood block, and with a sharp axe he chopped choice pieces of the meat and bone into the five-gallon tin bucket that served as a dog pot. He returned what was left of the porcupine to the cabin roof, out of reach of the dogs. Later that evening he cooked the meat and bones, thickening the broth with cornmeal to make a stout, rich porridge. When done, the brew was set aside to cool for the night; it was fed to the dogs next day.

In the years that followed that afternoon, living the woods life in all its varied fullness, I burned my score of porcupines. I built my fire of sticks in the yard and singed the quills, beating them off with a stick in the way I had learned, while my own dogs sat by and watched.

The thick, muscular tail of the porcupine particularly was a great source of fat meat, and a full-grown carcass would last for several days. While it was cooking, the meat smelled strong, a mingling of burned hair and fire-scorched hide. But after a while that smell became almost pleasant, concentrated and potent as it rose from the steaming pot in which the cornmeal bubbled with meat and fat.

Barbaric if you say so, but religious too in a strangely appropriate way, the quill-burning was one of the rites by which we lived and kept the seasons. I look back on it as an occasional sacrifice before the memory of a long-ago woods-spirit, the details of which were spare and essential: the brush fire kindled, the acrid white and yellow smoke spilling upward from the burned quills, the big pot sitting by, and the clean axe waiting. The smell of singed porcupine, the heavy, rich odor of the simmering broth lingered about the house and yard for days.

Three Days

I

SIX O'CLOCK ON A JANUARY MORNING. I wake, look into the darkness overhead, and then to the half-lighted windows. I listen. No sound comes to me from the world outside. The wind is quiet.

I get out of bed, pulling the stiffness from my body. Jo is still sleeping under the big down robe, turned toward the wall. I go to the window with a flashlight and look out at the thermometer. It is minus thirty-one, clear, and no moon. It will not be light for another three hours.

I put on a jacket and pair of slippers, and go outside. The door creaks on its frosty hinges, the latch is cold to my hand. One of our dogs emerges from his house in the yard and shakes himself, rattling his chain.

The stars are bright, Orion gone down to the west. The Dipper has turned, Arcturus above the hill. The sky and the snow give plenty of light, and I can easily see the outlines of the river channel below the house, and the dark crests of the hills around me. The air is sharp and clean, it will be a good day.

I gather up a few sticks of wood from the porch and go back indoors. Laying the wood on the floor beside the stove, I go to a table by the south window, find a match, and light the lamp. I turn the wick up slowly, letting the chimney warm.

Light gathers in the room, reflecting from the window glass

58

and the white enamel of a washpan. I open the stove door and the damper in the pipe. With a long poker I reach into the big firebox and rake some of the hot coals forward. I lay kindling on them, dry slivers of spruce, and two or three dry sticks on top of these. I close the door and open the draft. Air sucks through the draft holes, and in no time the fire is burning, the wood crackling. I fill the big kettle with water from a bucket near at hand, and set it on the back of the stove. It will soon be singing.

By now Jo is awake and beginning to function. I sit on the edge of the bed, putting thoughts together. The lamp makes shadows in the small room; heat is beginning to flow from the stove.

Today I am going back to our cabin below Banner Dome to look at my traps. I have not been out for over a week, and must surely have caught something by now. While Jo makes breakfast, I begin to dress. We talk a little; the mornings here are quiet, the days also.

I put on heavy wool trousers over my underwear, and two wool shirts. Over the wool trousers I sometimes wear another light cotton pair to break the wind or to keep off the snow. I put on socks—three pair of wool, and the felt oversock; two pair of insoles, and last the moosehide moccasins. I tie them at the top; they are a loose fit, soft and light on my feet. I made them six years ago from the hide of a big moose, and though worn by now, they are still the best I have.

I go out to the storehouse, find my big basket, and begin to pack. I will need my small axe, a few traps, and perhaps a few snares. That piece of dried moose paunch I have been saving—it is strong smelling and will make good bait. What else? Something needed for the cabin—a candle, some kerosene in a bottle. I put it all together in the basket.

We eat our breakfast slowly, there is no hurry. Half-frozen blueberries with milk, oatmeal, bread, and plenty of coffee. We listen to the stove, to the kettle buzzing. How many winters have gone by like this? Each morning that begins in the same quiet way—the darkness, the fire, the lamp, the stirring within. We talk a little, what she will do when I am gone. Food will have to be cooked for the dogs, there is plenty of wood. I am not sure when I will return; in three days, maybe.

By seven-thirty I am ready. I get my stuff together—into the basket now goes a light lunch, some bread for the cabin. I put on my old green army parka with its alpaca lining buttoned into it. It is heavily patched, and by now almost a homemade thing, the hood sewn large and trimmed with fur to shield my face from the wind. I take two wool caps, one for my head, and another in the basket in case I should need it. My big mittens also go into the pack; to start with, I will need only a pair of canvas gloves.

I say good-bye at the door, and walk up the hill. The dogs think that they may be going too, and the four of them begin to bark, waiting for the harness and tugging at their chains. But today I am going on foot; I want to take my time, to look around and set new traps. My dogs are too much in a hurry.

I begin the long climb through the birchwood to the ridge. The trail goes steeply the first few hundred yards, but it soon takes an easier grade, turning north and away from the river. The woods are still dark, but there is light in the snow, and perhaps a brightening in the sky above the trees. Morning and evening come on slowly this time of year, a gradual twilight. I carry a light walking stick made of birch in one hand as I go along. It comes in handy, to knock snow off the brush, to test the ice when I cross a creek, or to kill an animal with when I find one alive in a trap.

It is a winter of light snowfall, with barely ten inches on the ground, and I do not need my snowshoes. The trail is packed hard underfoot, and is easy walking, but away in the woods the snow is still loose and powdery under a thin crust; in the dim light I see that it is littered with dry, curled leaves and small, winged seeds from the alders and birches.

The air is sharp on my face, and it pinches my nose, but I soon begin to feel warm from climbing. I open my parka and push the cap back on my head; I take off my gloves and put them into one of my pockets. It won't do to get overheated.

Behind me now I hear an occasional mournful howl from one of our dogs, sunken and distant in the timber. Otherwise, there is not a sound in the woods this morning, and no air moving in the trees; but now and then the quiet snap of something contracting or expanding in the frost. At other times I have walked this trail in deep snow and bright moonlight, when the birch shadows made another transparent forest on the snow. There were shadows within the shadows, and now and then something would seem to move there—rabbit or lynx, or only a shape in my mind.

Partway up the hill I come to a marten set. Earlier in the season I caught a marten here, close to home, but there is nothing in the trap this morning. In the grey light I see that nothing has come to it, and all the tracks in the snow around it are old.

Frost bristles on the trap, a dense white fur over the jaws, the pan, and the trigger. I put my gloves back on, spring the trap, and bang it a couple of times against the pole to knock the frost from it.

I have two ways of setting traps for marten—one on the snow, and the other on a pole above the snow. This is a pole set. To make it, I have cut down a young birch four feet above the snow, and drawn the trunk of the tree forward a couple of feet to rest in the vee of the stump. I split the end of it to take a piece of bait, and the trap is set back a short space on top of the pole and held in place with a piece of light wire or string. It is a good way in heavy snow; once caught, the marten will always be found hanging from the pole.

Satisfied that the trap is working properly, I reset it, tying the wire loosely in place again. I go on, walking at a steady pace as the trail levels and climbs, winding among the birches.

Within half an hour I come out of the trees and into the open on the long, cleared ridge that rises behind the homestead. Light is stronger here, and I can see the cold, blue height of Banner Dome to the north beyond a range of hills. I have a long ways to go.

I begin to cool off now that I am on top, so I wear my gloves and button the front of my parka. As I stride along in the lightly drifted snow, I savor once more the cold stillness of this winter morning—my breath blown in a long plume before me, and no sound but the soft crunch of my moccasins, and the grating of my stick in the snow.

This ridge like a true watershed divides what I like to think of as my country; for in a way I own it, having come by it honestly, and nearly its oldest resident now. To the south of me, all the way down to the river, it is mostly dry hillside with birch and aspen. To the north, falling way into Redmond and Banner creeks, it is spruce country, mossy and wet. Years ago, when I first lived here, this ridge was heavily wooded; the trail wound through the timber, companionable and familiar, with small clearings and berry patches. Then, eight years ago, came a pipeline crew clearing the ridges and hillsides into Fairbanks. And later they built a power line to run beside it, from Fairbanks to Delta. The cleared way is overgrown with grass, with alders and raspberries, and the pipe is buried in the ground; but the ridge is windy now, and the trail drifts badly in heavy snow. Because of this, few fur animals come here, and I have no traps on this ridge.

I see some much-trampled snow at the edge of the timber, and turn aside to look. Moose have been feeding here at night, and the tops of many of the smaller trees are pulled down, broken, and bitten. I find a couple of hard-packed beds in the snow, and piles of black, frozen droppings. The moose must be close by, but they are out of sight, bedded down in the timber. I stand very still and listen, but hear nothing.

I cover a good mile of steady walking as the light grows and the snow brightens; the trail visible now some distance ahead of me where it follows the open ridge, paced by the power poles, dipping and curving with the slope of the hills. And then near the top of the last rise of hill the trail swings sharply north, and I go down into the woods again. The country changes swiftly, becomes dense and shaggy, the scrubby black spruce dominant, with alder and a few scattered birches. The trail is narrow, rutted, and uneven to walk. There is more snow here on a north slope, and I soon see marten sign, their characteristic tracks crossing my trail at intervals.

I have gone only a short distance when I find a marten dead in a trap. It is frozen, hanging head down at the end of the trap chain—a female, small, and with dull orange splashes over its neck and shoulders, a grizzled mask on its frost-pinched face. I release it from the trap and put the hard, stiff body in my pack. I cut a fresh piece of bait and reset the trap—where one marten has been caught, the chances are good for another.

Encouraged by my luck and in good spirits, I go on, following the trail through the woods, turning and climbing, past windfalls and old, rotted fire-stumps under the snow. A small covey of spruce hens startles me, flying up from the snow into the trees with a sudden flurry of wings. I hear an alarmed clucking, and see one of the big black and grey birds perched on a spruce bough, sitting very still but watching me with one bright eye.

On a point of hill where a stand of birches form an open grove, I stop for a short time to rest and reset a trap. The sun is up now, just clearing the hills to the south. There is light in the trees, a gold light laid on the blue and white of the snow, and luminous shadows. Frost crystals glitter in the still air wherever a shaft of sunlight pierces the forest.

This hill is open to the north, and I can see, closer now, the rounded summit of Banner Dome, rose and gold in the low sunlight. The Salchaket hills rising beyond it stand out clearly in the late-morning sunlight. I can just see part of the shoulder of hill that rises above the cabin I am going to, six miles yet by this trail. The valleys of Redmond and Glacier creeks lie below me, still in a deep, cold shadow. The sun will not reach there for another month.

I keep a cache on this hill, a fifty-gallon oil drum with a tight lid bolted to it. I brought it here on the sled a couple of years ago, on the last snow of the season. It stands upright between two birches, with its rusty grey paint a little out of place here in the woods, but to me familiar. Inside it I keep a few traps, a spare axe, and some cans of emergency rations in case I should need them. Whatever I leave there stays dry and is safe from bears.

I stand with my pack off for a moment, leaning on my stick. A little wind from somewhere stirs in the birches overhead. I have sometimes thought of building a small camp here, a shelter under these trees. There are places we are attracted to more than others, though I do not always know why. Here, it is the few strong birches, the airy openness of the woods, the view, and the blueberry shrubs under the trees where in good years we have come to pick them. If I were to begin again in some more distant part of the country, to build a home, this is one place I would consider. Perhaps because I know it so well, it is already part of what I think of as home.

I take up my pack and stick, ready to go on. I have put on my mittens, finally; my gloves have gotten damp and become icy and stiff on my hands. From here the trail descends the long north slope into Redmond, a wandering, downhill track through stubby open spruce and over much boggy ground, the longest hill I have to walk. As soon as I start down I am out of the sunlight and into shadow again. It feels at once colder, with a chill blue light in the snowy hummocks.

It is six years now since I cut this part of the trail, and it is worn deep in the moss from our summer walking. So little snow this winter, it makes hard foot and sled travel over the humps and holes. So I walk, going from one side of the trail to the other, springing from hummock to hummock, and balancing myself with my stick. I go at a good pace, anxious to cover the remaining ground before the day is over.

I am halfway down the hill when I find another marten in a trap set on the snow under a spruce. The marten is still alive, tugging at the end of the trap chain, angry and snarling. For a moment I stand and look at the animal. No larger than a house cat, but supple and snaky in body, it lunges at me as if it would bite me.

I take off my pack and approach the marten with my stick. I hit it a sharp blow across its nose, and it falls twitching in the snow. I quickly turn it on its back, lay my stick across its throat, and hold it there with one foot, while I place my other foot on its narrow chest. I can feel the small heart beating through the sole of my moccasin.

As I stand bending over it, the marten partly revives and attempts to free itself, kicking and squirming. But in a short time its heart stops and the slim body relaxes. I remove my foot and the stick, open the trap jaws, and lay the marten out in the snow. It is a large, dark male with thick fur.

It is better to find them dead and frozen, I do not like to kill them this way. Mostly they do not live long when caught in a trap in cold weather; another few hours, and this one too would have frozen.

I reset the trap at the bottom of the tree, placing it on two small dry sticks. I arrange the toggle stick so that the marten will have to step over it and into the trap. I cut a fresh piece of moose gut, and with my axe head I nail it to the tree a foot above the trap. To shield the bait from birds, I break off large twigs of spruce and stand them in the snow around the trap, but leave a small opening for the marten. Finally, I gather some fresh dry snow in the palm of my mitten and sprinkle it around the trap. Thinking that it will do, I put the dead marten into my basket, and go on my way, walking downhill into the cold bottom of Redmond.

The day passes, another hour, another mile. I walk, watching the snow, reading what is written there, the history of the tribes of mice and voles, of grouse and weasel, of redpoll and chickadee, hunter and prey. A scurry here, a trail ended there—something I do not understand, and stop to ponder. I find a trap sprung and nothing in it. I catch another marten, another male, so dark it is almost black. I am in luck today.

Already sunlight is fading from the hilltops. I look at my watch—it is past one, and I still have a good three miles to go. The air feels much colder here in this boggy creek bottom. I do not have a thermometer, but I judge it to be at least in the mid-thirties. There is some ice fog in this valley, a thin haze in the air above the creek, and that is always a sign of cold and stagnant air.

The trail is slick in places where spring water has seeped up through the snow and frozen into a pale yellow ice. We call it "overflow" or "glaciering," and it is common here in winter. I watch carefully while crossing; the ice is firm, but where ice and snow meet, a little water sometimes steams in the cold air. I feel with my stick as I go, suspecting more water under the snow.

At times while traveling like this, absent in mind or misjudging the snow, I have broken through thin ice and plunged halfway to my knees in slushy water. I have always climbed out quickly, and with so many socks on my feet I have never been wet to my skin. All the same, there is some danger in it, and I do not want to walk the rest of a day with frozen socks and trousers and icy moccasins. Today I am careful, and only once, while crossing a short stretch of overflow, do I look behind me and see water seeping into my tracks from the thin snow.

Twilight comes on slowly across the hills and through the forest; there are no more shadows. I stop again in a stand of spruce above the crossing on Glacier Creek. I have been feeling hungry for some time, so I nibble a frozen cookie from my pack. I have no water to drink, but I remove one of my mittens, and with the warm, bare hand ball up some snow until it is ice, and suck it.

Five years ago we camped here in a tent while hunting moose. That was before we built the cabin, and before I had cut a trail across the creek. The four dogs were with us, tied here among the trees. It was late in the fall, and below zero much of the time, but the tent with its big canvas fly and sheet-iron stove was warm enough. The tent poles still stand here, ready for use, and our cache is still here, a rough platform built into the trees eight feet above me.

I put the three marten I have caught in a sack, tie it, and hang it from a spike high in the cache. I will pick them up on my way home.

I take my pack and go off downhill to the creek—there is no water on the ice, and I am across safely and dry. Then on through the woods and through the swamp, across a low saddle between two hills, tired now, and glad to be getting to the end of it. Fresh marten sign in the snow, and one more marten caught.

I am within half a mile of the cabin, when I find a lynx alive in a marten trap. It has not been caught long, the toes of one big fore-foot barely held in the small steel jaws. The animal backs away from me, crouched and growling, its big tawny eyes fastened upon me, and its tufted ears laid back.

I take off my pack, approach carefully, and when I am close enough I hit the lynx hard on its head with my stick. Stunned, the animal sags in the snow. I turn the stick and hit it again with the heavier end, and strike it again, until the lynx sprawls and relaxes, and I am sure that it is dead. For so large an animal, they are easy to kill, but I wait to be certain—I do not want it coming alive in my hands.

Sure that it is dead, I release it from the trap. It is a big male, pale, and a choice fur. I hang the trap in a tree and shoulder my pack. Pleased with this unexpected catch, I drag the big lynx by one hind foot the rest of the way to the cabin, leaving a thread of blood behind me in the snow.

II

The cabin is hidden in a dense stand of spruce on a bench overlooking a small, brushy creek. The creek has no name on the maps, but I have called it Cabin Creek for the sake of this camp. The ground is perhaps 1,700 feet in elevation, and from the cabin I can look up and see the clear slope of Banner Dome another thousand feet above.

With its shed roof sloping north, the cabin sits low and compact in the snow, a pair of moose antlers nailed above a window in the high south wall. There are four doghouses to the rear of it, each of them roofed with a pile of snow-covered hay. A meat rack stands to one side, built high between two stout spruces, and a ladder made of dry poles leans against a tree next to it. A hindquarter of moose hangs from the rack; it is frozen rock hard and well wrapped with canvas to keep it from birds. Just the same, I see that camp-robbers have pecked at it and torn a hole in the canvas. Nothing else can reach it there, seven feet above the ground.

Nothing has changed since I was last here, and there has been no new snow. Squirrel and marten tracks are all around the cabin, and some of them look fresh; I must set a trap somewhere in the yard.

I leave the dead lynx in the snow beside the cabin; I will skin it later. I lean my walking stick by the door and ease the pack from my shoulders—I am a little stiff from the long walk, and it feels good to straighten my back. A thermometer beside the door reads thirty below.

I open the door, go inside, and set my pack down by the bunk. The cabin is cold, as cold as the outdoors, but there is birch bark and kindling by the stove, and I soon have a fire going. The small sheet-iron stove gets hot in a hurry; I watch the pipe to see that it does not burn.

As the cabin warms up I take off my parka, shake the frost from it, and hang it from a hook near the ceiling. The last time I was here I left a pot of moose stew on the floor beside the stove. Now I lift the pot and set it on the edge of the stove to thaw.

I will need water. Much of the time here I scoop up buckets of clean snow to melt on the stove. There is not much water in a bucketful of dry snow, even when the snow is packed firm, and many buckets are needed to make a gallon or two of water. But this year the snow is shallow, and it is dirty from the wind, with dust and twigs and cones from the trees around the cabin.

And so while the light stays I take a bucket and an ice chisel, and go down to a small pond below the cabin. Under the snow the ice is clear, and in a short time I chop enough of it to fill the bucket. There is water under the ice, but I know from past use of it that the ice itself is cleaner and has a fresher taste.

Before going back up to the cabin I stand for a moment and take in the cold landscape around me. The sun has long gone, light on the hills is deepening, the gold and rose gone to a deeper blue. The cold, still forest, the slim, black spruce, the willows and few gnarled birches are slowly absorbed in the darkness. I stand here in complete silence and solitude, as alone on the ice of this small pond as I would be on the ice cap of Greenland. Only far above in the blue depth of the night I hear a little wind on the dome.

I stir myself and begin walking back up the hill to the cabin with my bucket of ice. Before it is dark completely I will want to get in more wood. There are still a few dry, standing poles on the slope behind the cabin, and they are easy to cut. There will be time for that.

Past three o'clock, and it is dark once more. I am done with my chores. Inside the cabin I light a kerosene lamp by the window, and hang my cap and mittens to dry above the stove. The ice has half-melted in the bucket, and the stew is hot and steaming. I have eaten little this day, and I am hungry. I put on the kettle for tea, set out a plate, and cut some bread. The stew is thick and rich; I eat it with the bread and cold, sweetened cranberries from a jar beneath the table.

Fed and feeling at ease, I sit here by the window, drinking tea, relaxing in the warmth of the cabin. The one lamp sends a soft glow over the yellow, peeled logs. When we built this cabin I set the windows low in the walls so that we could look out easily while sitting. That is the way of most old cabins in the woods, where windows must be small and we often sit for hours in the winter, watching the snow. Now I look out the double panes of glass; there is nothing to see out there but the warm light from the window falling to the snow. Beyond that light there is darkness.

I get up from my chair to put another stick of wood in the stove and more water in the kettle. I am tired from the long walk, and sleepy with the warmth and food. I take off my moccasins and lie down on the bunk with a book, one of a half-dozen I keep here. It is Virgil's *Aeneid*, in English. I open the book to the beginning of the poem and read the first few lines. Almost immediately I fall asleep. When I wake up, it is nearly six o'clock; the fire has burned down and the cabin is chilly.

I feel lazy and contented here with nothing urgent to do, but I get up anyway and feed more wood to the stove. On my feet again, moving around, I find that I am still hungry—all day out in the cold, one uses a lot of fuel. So I heat up what remains of the stew and finish it off. Tomorrow I will cut more meat from the quarter hanging outside, and make another pot. What I do not eat, I will leave here to freeze for another day.

Having eaten and rested, I feel a surge of energy. I go outside to bring in the lynx, intending to skin it; I don't want to carry that heavy carcass home. The lynx is already stiff, beginning to freeze. I carry it in and lay it on the floor near the stove to thaw, while I make myself another cup of tea. When I can move its legs easily, I pull one of the big hind feet into my lap and begin to cut with my pocketknife below the heel where the foot pad begins. The skin is stiff and cold under thick fur as it comes slowly free from the sinew.

But soon in the warmth of the room I begin to see fleas, red fleas, crawling out of the fur. One of them, suddenly strong, jumps onto me, and then to the bunk. That is enough. I put down my knife and take the lynx back outdoors. I will leave it here to freeze, and when I come again the fleas will be dead. I am in no hurry about it, and I do not want fleas in my clothing and in my bunk. Already I begin to itch.

Outside, I leave the lynx in the snow once more, and for a brief time I stand in front of the cabin, to watch and listen. The cold air feels good on my bare skin. The stars are brilliant—Polaris and the Dipper overhead. Through a space in the trees to the south I can see part of the familiar winter figure of Orion, his belt and sword; in the north I see a single bright star I think is Vega. I hear an occasional wind-sigh from the dome, and now and then moving air pulls at the spruces around me.

What does a person do in a place like this, so far away and alone? For one thing, he watches the weather—the stars, the snow, and the fire. These are the books he reads most of all. And everything that he does, from bringing in firewood and buckets of snow, to carrying the waste water back outdoors, requires that he stand in the open, away from his walls, out of his man-written books and his dreaming head for a while. As I stand here, refreshed by the stillness and closeness of the night, I think it is a good way to live.

But now the snow is cold through my stocking feet, and I go back indoors. I wash the dishes and clean the small table, putting things away for the night. I hang up my trousers and wool shirts, and hang my socks on a line near the ceiling. There is still some hot water in the kettle; I pour it into a basin, cool it with a cup of cold water from the bucket, and wash my face and hands. Having dried myself and brushed my teeth, I am ready for bed.

Lying on the bunk once more, with the lamp by my left shoulder, I pick up my book and try to read again. A page, and then another. My mind fills with images: a fire in the night, Aeneas, and the flight from Troy. I drowse, then wake again. I remember Fred Campbell lying on his cot in the lake cabin that good fall many years ago, the Bible held overhead in his hand as he tried to read. And soon he was sleeping, the book fallen to his chest. The same page night after night. I was amused at him then, but older now I see the same thing happens to me. It is the plain life, the air, the cold, the hard work; and having eaten, the body rests and the mind turns to sleep.

I wake once more and put away my book. I get up from the bunk and bank the fire, laying some half-green sticks of birch on the coals, and close down the draft. Ice has melted in the bucket, there is plenty of water for the morning.

I blow out the lamp and settle down in the sleeping bag, pulling it around my shoulders. I look into the dark cabin, and to the starlight on the snow outside. At any time here, away from the river and the sound of traffic on the road, I may hear other sounds—a moose in the creek bottom, breaking brush, a coyote on a ridge a mile away, or an owl in the spruce branches above the cabin. Often it is the wind I hear, a whispering, rushy sound in the boughs. Only sometimes when the wind blows strongly from the south I hear a diesel on the road toward Fairbanks, changing gears in the canyon. And once, far away on a warm south wind, the sound of dogs barking at Richardson.

I spend another day at the cabin, taking my time. I loaf and read, cut more wood and chop some ice. I thaw and skin the one marten, and roll the fur in a sack to take with me; it will mean a pound or two less to carry, and more room in the basket. With the ladder and a block and tackle, I take down the moose quarter, unwrap it, and saw a piece of meat from the round. It was killed late and is not fat meat, but having hung frozen for so long it is tender enough. The outside of the meat is darkened and dried and will need to be trimmed. I put the piece I have cut on a board near the stove to thaw.

In the afternoon I go up the creek to look at some snares I have set there. I find that nothing has come but one lynx, and he pushed a snare aside. It may have been the one I caught.

From the creek I climb a couple of miles up the ridge toward the dome. It is easy walking in the light snow, and here on higher ground there is bright sunlight and the air seems to be warmer. There is plenty of marten sign in the open spruce mixed with aspen, and I set two traps.

I mark the days on a calendar, drawing a circle around the dates. The calendar shows a ship, full rigged in the old romantic style of the sea, hard driven from Cape Horn, or following the trades homeward. This calendar comes from Canada, and bears the trade name of *John Leckie & Company, Ltd., Edmonton, Alberta. Marine Supplies and Hardware.* Three years ago I bought a whitefish net from them by mail, and now each year they send me a calendar. Since we have others at home, I bring them here. They look fine against the log walls, and brighten their place by the window.

I remember how we built this cabin, the many hours here, the long walks in the rain that turned into snow. I had the big wall tent pitched in the woods, near where the cabin is now, a cot to sleep on, and the small iron stove with its pipe stuck through a piece of sheet metal in the tent roof. I would come here from home in the afternoons, packing some food, lumber, and tools. I worked on the cabin until dark, and slept overnight in the tent. Again the next morning, from the first light, I worked hard, trimming and fitting the logs, then walked home in the afternoon over the wet hills.

I worked from early August until mid-October, a few hours or a day at a time. Fall came early that year, and toward the end of it I was scraping frozen bark from the roof poles, determined to make a clean job of it. There was no dry sod for the roof, so we went to the creek to cut big batts of half-frozen moss and carry them up the hill one at a time. And finally we had a roof on the cabin, the door hung and windows fitted, and a fire in the stove.

That fall I shot a moose from the front of the cabin just at dusk. It was a long shot down into the flat below the hill, the moose only a dark shape in the frozen grass. Then came the work that evening and part of the next day, cutting the meat into quarters and dragging them up the hill to the camp. We hung the meat high on the rack I built that morning behind the cabin. We had a long walk home that afternoon in wet snow, carrying with us a chunk of the ribs, the tongue, the heart, the kidneys and liver. It was a hard fall, in many ways the hardest and poorest year I have spent in the North.

But the time and work was worth it, for here is the cabin now, snug and warm. No matter how long it stands here, it will always seem like a new thing, strange to come upon far in these hills at the end of a long hike, and to know we have built it.

I look around me, at the floor, at the walls, at the ceiling, the logs and poles. When the cabin was first built we had only hay for a floor, a deep bed of it spread on the moss. There was nothing to sweep or to clean, and each fall I brought in a few armloads of new hay to freshen the floor. But as cheery and rustic as it was, there were things about that hay floor I never liked. Frost was deep in the ground beneath the hay, and because the cabin went unoccupied for many weeks in winter, it was cold and damp to live in until the fire had thawed it. Mice and squirrels tunneled through the moss and into the cabin, and made a mess in the bedding. And so one spring before the trail went soft, I brought sledloads of lumber here. In August of that year I came and worked three days, putting in a proper floor. Now it is dry and warm, and the mice stay out. I sweep it now and then.

There is only the one room, eight feet by twelve feet, but it is large enough for a camp in the woods. The door opens west, and the two windows face north and south. Overhead I have cut a round hole in one wall for a vent, and fitted it with a metal lid. The peeled poles of the ceiling are still clean and bright yellow; smoke has not darkened them and the roof has never leaked.

Here at the back of the room I have built two bunks, one above the other, with a small ladder at one end to reach the upper. The table I eat from and the work table across the room are both fashioned from two-inch wooden pegs driven into auger holes in the logs. Boards are laid across the pegs and nailed in place. The few shelves are made in the same way. It is a simple means of making the essential furniture, and there are no table legs to get in the way underfoot.

Here and there I have driven nails and spikes into the walls; some odds and ends of clothing hung there, a few traps, a piece of rope. A .22 rifle is propped on a couple of spikes at the foot of the lower bunk. Behind the stove hang pots and washpans, and into one log by the door I have driven a twelve-inch spike from which I hang the dog harness to dry.

There have been other winters here, not easy ones. I have come after a heavy snowfall, with the dogs dead-tired and me walking behind or in front of the sled, breaking trail. We were five or six hours getting here, the traps buried, something caught but hard to find in the snow. And then would come the journey home the next day over a soft, half-broken trail with a load of meat and three dogs; me again walking behind, steering, holding the snubline while the dogs pulled ahead.

Fifty years ago in the twilight of the gold rush, wagon roads and freight trails were still in use here. Although they are badly overgrown now and deeply rutted, I can still walk parts of them for a short distance; they go up the creek, across the divide and down Shamrock, to the Salcha River and Birch Lake, many miles from here. It is strange to think of it then, the country still busy with people coming and going, the dogs and horses, freight and men.

No one comes here now but Jo and myself, the dogs and us, the moose and the marten. Only once, three years ago, two men came from Banner Creek with a Cat to prospect on Glacier Creek, two miles over the hill. They cleared a small piece of ground on the beach above the creek, but they found nothing there and did not come back. I am glad of that, I like having this country to myself.

I am living out a dream in these woods. Old dreams of the Far North, old stories read and absorbed: of snow and dogs, of moose and lynx, and of all that is still native to these unpeopled places. Nothing I have yet done in life pleases me as much as this. And yet it seems only half deliberate, as if I had followed a scent on the wind and found myself in this place. Having come, I will have to stay, there's no way back.

The hunting and fishing, the wild fruit, the trapping, the wood that we burn and the food that we eat—it is all given to us by the country. The fur of this marten is lovely when held in the light, shaken so that the hair stands from the pelt. And meat of the moose is good to have; it keeps us fed and warm inside, and I pay no butcher for it. Yet I cannot trap and kill without thought or emotion, and it may be that the killing wounds me also in some small but deadly way. Life is here equally in sunlight and frost, in the thriving blood and sap of things, in their decay and sudden death.

It can be hard and cruel sometimes, as we are prepared to see it clearly. I put the beast to death for my own purposes, as the lynx kills the rabbit, the marten the squirrel, and the weasel the mouse. Life is filled with contradictions—confused and doubting in the heart of a man, or it is straight as an arrow and full of purpose.

I look at my hands and flex my fingers. They have handled much, done things I hardly dreamed of doing when I was younger. I have woven my nets with them and made my snares. I have pulled the trigger of my rifle many times and watched a bird fall or a moose crumple to the ground. And with these hands I have gone deep into the hot body of the animal, and torn from it the still-quivering tissue of lungs, heart, liver, and guts. There is blood under the nails, dirt and grease in the cracks of the finger joints.

I have learned to do these things, and do them well, as if I'd come into something for which I had a native gift. And a troubling thought will return sometimes: having done so much, would I kill a man? I do not know. I might if I had to, in anger, perhaps, passion of defense or revenge. But not, I think, in the cold, judging light of the law. I have seen a war, a dead man floating in the sea off a Pacific island, and I was there. By my presence alone, I took part in many deaths. I cannot pretend that I am free and guiltless. Justice evades us; the forest with all its ancient scarcity and peril is still within us, and it may be that we will never know a world not haunted in some way by a return to that night of the spirit where the hangman adjusts his noose and the executioner hones his axe to perfection.

I put these thoughts away, and look out the window to the sun-lit snow on the hillside across the creek. In this wilderness life I have found a way to touch the world once more. One way. To live the life that is here to be lived, as nearly as I can without that other—clock hands, hours, and wages. I relive each day the ancient expectation of the hunt—the setting out, and the trail at dawn. What will we find today?

I leave some of my mankindness behind me for a while and become part tree, a creature of the snow. It is a long way back, and mostly in shadow. I see a little there, not much, but what I see will never be destroyed.

I may not always be here in these woods. The trails I have made will last a long time; this cabin will stand twenty years at least before it falls. I can imagine a greater silence, a deeper shadow where I am standing, but what I have loved will always be here.

Night, and the day passes. Evening, another pot of stew—rice and chunks of meat, dried vegetables, onions, a little fat, and spice for flavor. The weather holding steady, still twenty-nine below. I continue to hear some wind on the dome.

I rise early on the morning of the third day, make my breakfast by lamplight. Oats and bread, some meat in the frying pan. Might as well feed up, it will be another long day. I take my time this morning, dressing slowly, putting things away. I bring in more wood and stack it by the stove. Outside in the clear frost I hang the frozen lynx high on the rack; nothing will bother it there. Dawn comes slowly over the hills, lighting the snowy dome.

I pack my gear—the small axe again, a few traps. One marten skin to carry, three marten to pick up on the way. My pack will be as heavy as before.

The fire slowly dies and the cabin grows cool again. I fill a shallow pan with the remaining water and place it on the stove. It will freeze, and I will have water quickly the next time here. I put away my saw and the big axe; there is bark and kindling at hand when I come again. I close the door and latch it. I look around with care, at the cabin and the yard—everything is in place. I will be back in a week or ten days.

It is minus twenty-four degrees this morning; some thin clouds are forming, it may snow by evening. I take my pack and, stick in hand, set off up the trail toward Glacier Creek.

III

It is evening again, and I have come home by the river from Banner Creek. I came by another trail today, over the long divide between Redmond and Banner, another part of the country. It was hard walking in places; much of it is steep side-hill scraped and gouged by a Cat trail made many years ago, with several small springs and water under the snow.

I met with some wind on a high and open ridge where I could look east into the rose-grey morning sunlight. I felt too warm from climbing, and stopped to take the lining out of my parka. The wind came only now and then, not cold, a little loose snow blowing across the open trail.

Few traps and no marten there, but plenty of moose sign in the willows going down into Banner. One big red fox caught somehow in a trap set for marten, caught by the toes only, and not for long. He watched me as I came near, stretched out on the short chain, his eyes enormous with alertness and fear. I thought of trying to knock him out with a blow from my stick, so that I could free him from the trap and let him go. But I finally killed him, breaking his neck as I have learned to do. I put him into my pack with the others, tying him down, and took the trap with me.

I was close to Banner Creek, walking slowly on a straight and open stretch of the trail, when I came upon a set of wolf tracks. They were soon joined by others, and I saw that two, possibly three wolves had come out of the dense, sloping sprucewood to the north, and finding my foot trail, had turned to follow it.

Thinking they might return in a few days, I set two heavy snares in that open place, a few yards apart from each other. I propped the nooses over my trail, supporting them with some brush cut from the woods close by and stuck down in the scant snow. I tried to make the sets appear as natural as I could, and looking at them afterwards from a distance, it seemed to me that they might work. Yet somehow I do not expect much from them; the wind may blow them down, or the wolves go around them.

I went on down Banner Creek, walking the old road between the spruce and the birch, the snow so light this winter it hardly fills the frozen ruts. A side path turning off into the woods brought me into a brushy flat where I keep an ancient and tilting cabin. I stopped there to build a fire in the stove and make some tea. My feet were sore from walking that hard trail in soft moccasins, and it felt good to take off the pack and rest for a while. The cabin is old and damp and does not heat well, but it is better than no camp at all.

Afterwards I searched the brushed-in trails near the cabin where I have set snares for lynx. But I have caught nothing there this winter. Today one snare was missing; something had made off with it—what? The snow told me nothing.

In late afternoon I walked the last mile home along the Tanana, through the woods on the steep hillside between the river and the highway. The sun was gone, and light on the river, on the ice, a steely grey. Clouds were building a heavy darkness in the west. Sounds came to me along the river: water running somewhere out on the ice, a dog barking at Richardson. A car went by on the road, going to Fairbanks, going to Delta. People.

I sit here now, the long day over and the pack gone from my shoulders at last. My heavy clothing removed, moccasins hung up to dry, gloves and mittens drying on the rack above the stove. Half-sleepy, warmed by the fire, while Jo makes supper, and we talk. What happened while I was gone? Yesterday, today, the day before. A moose on the hill, water and wood, and no one came. The world is still the same, it will be the same tomorrow.

I am happy deep inside. Not the mind-tiredness of too much thought, of thoughts that pursue each other endlessly in that forest of nerves, anxiety, and fear. But a stretching kind of tiredness, the ease and satisfaction of the time well spent, and of the deep self renewed.

Tomorrow, marten to skin and meat to cut. What else? It is two degrees below zero this evening. The wind is blowing.

Spring

THE SUN IS WARM IN MY YARD this spring afternoon. It is the first clear day without wind. I am sitting on the sawhorse, doing nothing. Looking out over the Tanana River, looking at the ground, watching and thinking. My mind sleeps and awakens. I think how good the sun feels on my back and shoulders. Good-bye to so much darkness and frost, to the long night. I watched the sun barely clear a mountain in the south; its spent light without heat threw long, blue shadows over the snow. And then the days slowly lengthened and brightened.

The sun has come back. It has been a good winter after all, with little snow after the first deep fall in October. A warm winter. For a few days in January the temperature fell to thirty-five and forty below. After that the wind blew, a mighty and blustering force out of the south, sweeping across the hills, shaking the birches; the deep cold was gone. Now, in April, meltwater seeps and drips from every cornice and clay bank, and pools of water deepen in the yard.

Flies buzz around me, their green bodies shining in the sunlight. They light on the woodpile, and on the wall of the house nearby, drawn there by the warmth. If a shadow passes over them, they move away into the light again. Flies awakened early this spring, trapped behind the glass of the storm windows. They fumed and droned there, to die or sleep again. A little sunlight, some warmth finding its way into the house walls, and they return to life. After long silence they are welcome.

I watch a carpenter ant crawl about on a chunk of split firewood at my feet. The wood is dry spruce from an old snag up the creek. The ant has lived there all winter in the honeycomb passages. Now he is out here in this strange, new place of warmth and passing shadows. His black skeleton glistens in the light. He feels his way along.

Wet snow and sawdust underfoot. Wood dust from my saw fell here all winter under the sawhorse, mixing with the snow. Now the snow melts, and the sawdust settles in a sodden heap. If I push it aside with my boot, I see that it darkens toward the ground; it is turning slowly to soil itself.

An odor, strong and sharp with ammonia, comes off the low bank where my dogs are chained to their houses. It is too wet for them on the ground; they lie on top of their houses, blinking, sleeping in the sun. They too like this warmth and stillness.

All around me I see the debris of winter, long hidden by snow. The scattered woodchips, the gnawed bones; part of a moose jaw, a hoof, a lost spoon. Bits of trash, moose hair, peelings thrown out and forgotten; urine stains in the rotting snow. The ground smells sour.

This morning I worked in the greenhouse, loosening the soil, turning it over, setting it free to the sun and air. The plants I have cared for all spring stand here in their flats and boxes: tomatoes, peppers, and cucumbers; cabbages and broccoli. I took them from the house this morning to let them harden for a while outdoors. It will soon be time to set them in the garden.

Already the earth is warm where the snow has gone. Patches of dead grass have been visible for several days. I see a few green shoots there above the roots. Shoots of fireweed and wild rhubarb have begun to break through the banked soil by the porch. They are the first things up in the spring, good to eat until they grow tall and bitter.

I look away from my yard to the river glittering below me in the sunlight. There is ice yet in the channels, and drifts of snow on the islands. And far across to the south, much snow in the foothills.

But that too is melting, like the snow here in my yard and on the hillside above me. And soon water will be rushing down through the ditches, under the culverts and bridges, away downhill to the river. Water brown as tobacco, stained with tannin, strong to drink.

I know that ice is still thick on the creek below the house. Much overflow came last winter, the springwater seeping somehow through the frozen soil, flowing out over the ice and freezing again. It will take a long time to melt; there will be ice there in shaded places well into June. And back in the woods, on the sidehill, stumps of the birches I cut last winter are pink and wet. Sap is rising, flowing away into the soil again. At night it freezes over the stumps in a glaze of clear, pink ice.

I hear geese out there on the river bars, small groups of them wherever there is bare soil and open water. Last night I heard them flying through the darkness overhead; the sound came to me in my sleep. Snow buntings have passed through and flown west, like flocks of small, black and white pigeons wheeling over the snowfields. I have seen longspurs and rosy finches on the roadside toward Delta, picking seed and gravel, bursting away as the cars approach. They are bound west and north to the open tundra and the high, bare summits.

I found a butterfly this morning, the first one I have seen this year. I found it resting on the wet, half-frozen road, motionless in shadow. I knew it for a mourning cloak: the brown and violet, smoky darkness of its wings, their pale flame-edges pulsing. I picked it up and held it in the sunlight, warming it with my breath, until its wings loosened and it flew away.

To do nothing, to be nothing: that would be a good life. Be still, like a stone in the sun. All this running after life, this chasing of things: felling trees, cutting wood to keep warm, melting snow and ice for water; there is no end to it. Hunting down meat, hauling it home for miles with the sled and dogs; learning the ways of an animal in snow, that I may lift the fur from its back. Eating, washing, finding time to sleep; waking in the cold, half-light of dawn, hungry and thinking.

Our sleep is not long enough. How much better to be a bear, and snore from November through February, those months of darkness and uncertainty, when it seems that the world will never be warm again, that even the ravens must fall frozen from the sky, and chickadees and redpolls drop from the aspen twigs like feathery lumps of ice. To awaken again when the sun comes back, and water drips from the eaves. Sunlight in the mouth of the cave says it is time once more.

This clarity and distance and light. It is almost too much, the gift we have waited for, this loosening and freeing of the spirit. All things must feel it now; everything that was cold and gripped in darkness, shedding itself, bit by bit letting go, falling to the ground. I hear a sound like thunder, a heavy splash, as another half-acre of ice collapses on the river.

Two weeks more, and our fox sparrow will come again to the thicket below the house. He will sit on the same branch of the same birch, and sing the song he sang last summer. As long as I have lived here a fox sparrow has sung from that tree. Many generations of sparrows have nested there in the alder thicket and learned that song, a sweetness never forgotten.

I saw a cow moose on the hillside last evening, half-hidden in the reddish, twiggy growth of the birches. She will soon have a calf, perhaps more than one, and feed all summer along the river. There, in the sloughs and on the islands, she and her calf may be safe from bears. When snow has gone from the high country, the bulls will move to the upper slopes of Banner Dome, above timber. They will not be down again until late August.

A fly settles on my hand, then moves away. Soon the big, furry bumblebees will be fumbling the larkspur and fireweed blossoms. And all too soon the mosquitoes will come. First, the old ones wintered over from last fall. They are heavy and slow in flight, but they still want blood. Then, in the first week of June, the new crop, tiny and ferocious, swarming out of every ditch, pond, and pool of meltwater. For a few weeks life here in the woods will not always be pleasant. But now the air is mild and clear, and we can sit like this, soaking in the warmth and stillness. If a mosquito comes near us, solitary and wandering, we will brush him quietly away.

There is much to be done; it is nearly May, the buds on the poplars will be swollen and sticky. I have the garden to spade and plant, the greenhouse to heat and water. When all that is done, I will start work on a new boat. I have drawn a sketch for it, a rough plan. I will build it twenty feet long, narrow and flat-bottomed, with plenty of flare and a shovel nose. I am without money again this spring, but somehow the material will be found: a few boards and nails, some paint and tar. When the boat is built, I must find a new place to fish, perhaps upriver at the mouth of Tenderfoot. Last fall I watched the eddy there; it was deep and slow.

I can think of a thousand things, and some of them I may never do. I want to build a root cellar; not this year perhaps, but soon. Summer will be crowding me; the salmon will come in July, and for three weeks or so I will be busy packing and cleaning fish, and mending my nets. There will be berries to pick and wood to cut; the days drawing close again, the time for gathering up the garden and potatoes, as the year slopes down the far side of the summer. They will come soon enough, the hunting and the short days once more.

A shadow crosses my mind, and then it goes. The air feels cooler: a cloud shadow passes overhead, and a little wind comes off the river. I must bring my plants indoors. I move from where I have been sitting, and stretch like someone just awakened. I turn and look behind me toward the birchwood. I will be up there on the hillside soon, spading the ground for potatoes. A wind will blow from the northwest, a brief and chilling gust, bringing sleet and cold rain. But that will pass, and sunlight will be warm again. For a while, a few weeks, summer will stay.

Other Days

I T IS EVENING, EARLY IN NOVEMBER. I am sitting on the closed porch of the cabin at Richardson, making snares. Working with a few strands of cable and a pair of pliers, I make a sliding noose seven to eight inches in diameter; it will be for lynx, or coyote if I am lucky. The wire is tough and springy, and I find it hard to make the knots hold.

I have spent part of this day cutting wood. Out in the yard by the sawhorse there is a pile of freshly sawn birch, and slabs of it already split to be stacked against the outside wall of the cabin. The wood flesh, the sawdust and chips, are a pale yellow on the evening snow.

The cabin is warm; a fire smolders and sparks in the big black wood-range in the room behind me. Something is cooking there on the stovetop; the big kettle hums in the silence. Out the window, in the southwest, a cloudy light fades slowly over the mountains. The river channel at the foot of the hill is frozen, but downriver I see a dark streak in the snow: open water.

The land changes slowly in a thousand years. The river has shifted from one side of the valley to another, worn its bed deeper in the sediment and rock. Islands have formed, grown grass and willows, and then been washed away, to be drift-piles buried in sand. The spruce forest on these slopes gave way to fire, to birch and aspen, and in the spaces among these now the spruce come slowly back. The birch will die, stand punky, and fall, and moss thicken once more on the downed and rotting trunks.

Of all I can see from this hillside, the only recent things are the narrow roadway below the house and my own cluster of cabins and sheds. Everything else is as it has been for thousands of years. It was colder then, or warmer. Brown coal-beds were forming in the swamps to the south. Animals and birds very like those here now roamed the windy meadows, made their way south, and flew north again in a far springtime. Enormous herds left tracks in the snow, browsing the willows and lichens. And others no longer here, huger, with hairy sides and heavy tusks. They were hunted, pursued by shadows on the snow. They have passed through, they have eaten and killed.

Days and years run together. It is later and colder, past the middle of December, the shortest days. The sun has gone down behind Mount Deborah, a cold, pyramidal slab in the southwest. I am fitting together a new harness for the pup I am training. I have cut the leather from strips of tanned moose, made from the back of the animal, the thickest part of the hide. By the light of this window I sew the collar seams with an awl and heavy flax thread. I have already punched holes for the bellyband and the collar buckles.

A large piece of hide taken from a hindquarter of moose is soaking in a tub behind the stove. The hair has slipped, and I have scraped the hide clean. It soaks in a solution of soap and snow water. Stirred and wrung out once or twice a day, it will be ready in a week or two to be washed clean, then pulled and stretched until it is soft and dry. Later I will hang it in the smokehouse and smoke it with dry alder until it is a light or deeper brown. I will cut new moccasin soles from it.

I remember things. Names, friends of years past, a wife far off. Last week I saw a magazine article on contemporary painters in New York City, photographs of people I once knew. I wrote one of them a letter, telling of myself here in the North. There will be no answer, and all that seems very far and ages distant.

In that same magazine—or it was another sent to me, or borrowed from the roadhouse—I have read something of the politics of this nation and the world. Names again: Truman, MacArthur, Eisenhower, a place named Korea. But these too are distant and unreal. My life is here, in this country I have made, in the things I have built. In the world of Richardson and Tenderfoot, of Banner Creek, and the Tanana at the foot of the hill. I do not want more than this.

Winter comes dark and close; there is snow, and wind on the hills. It is a lean year, and there are few rabbits in the country now. Two years ago they were thick in the willows and alders; when snow went off in the spring, the gnawed bark showed pale near the height of the snowfall. Lynx followed the rabbits everywhere, and it was no trick at all to catch a dozen or so of the big cats in a few weeks' time. Now the snow in the woods shows little sign of anything, only dust and leaves, the occasional track of a fox or squirrel. I may catch a few marten on the ridges over behind Redmond Creek, a lynx in Banner flats, or a fox here along the river.

I have a small cabin at the mouth of Tenderfoot, six miles upriver. I built a new dogsled this fall, and I am eager to use it. I have dried fish stacked in the shed, potatoes and cabbage in the cellar, and wood in the yard. A moose, shot late and none too fat, hangs from the tall rack behind the cabin, frozen like a rock. Little by little I am learning the ways of the North. In the darkness and cold that is coming, we will not go hungry.

I put down my work; the light is poor, and I listen. A car drives slowly by and is gone over the hill. There are not many now so late in the year.

Seasons, years. The sun will rise over the hill next spring, the cold will come again, and more or less snow will fall. If I live here long enough, I may see a new migration of people from Asia. Here below me is the corridor, the way into the continent, a way still open until stopped once more by ice.

I am alone in my thirty-third year, strange to myself and the few people I know. In this immensity of silence and solitude, my childhood seems as distant as the age of mastodons and sloths; yet it is alive in me and in this life I have chosen to live. I am here and nowhere else.

It is dark in the cabin now, the fire in the stove is going out. I am done with these snares. I hang those I have finished on a nail by the doorway to the porch; I put away my tools and the lengths of unused wire. It is time to feed the dogs, and begin supper for myself. Tomorrow I must be up early, and out on the trail before light.

A breath of wind pulls smoke down across the south window. Out on the river, there is fog on that open water.

Wolves

THERE WERE WOLVES IN THE COUNTRY, but they too were more like shadows—a track now and then in the thin fall snow, a distant voice, a shape in the moonlight. There were not many of them in those years, the caribou having long since left that part of the country. Once they had been common, and I was told that Canyon Creek two miles west of the homestead had in early days been called Wolf Canyon because of the numbers of wolves that were sighted there. My old neighbor, Billy Melvin, swore to me that one night a large pack of wolves had gone down Banner Creek in deep snow, so many of them that the trail they left behind was firm enough to drive a team and sled over.

In mid-October of one year I killed a big moose on Cabin Creek, and left the four quarters cached upon a few poles and concealed under a heap of spruce brush. It was hard-freezing weather, and I had no fear of the meat spoiling. A few days later my wife and I and one of our dogs returned from home with a block and tackle to hang up the quarters. An inch of snow had fallen in the meantime, and everything that moved on foot left its mark to be seen.

Within three miles of the cache I found a large, fresh wolf track in our trail. It was joined by another, and then another. Three wolves were going before us, heading toward Cabin Creek. We walked on more quickly as we saw that their tracks remained steady in our trail. I began to worry that they would find our cache—in my imagination I saw our winter's meat exposed by the wolves, fouled and half eaten. Leaving the dog with my wife, I hurried on ahead as fast as I could with my pack and rifle, going nearly at a run over the frozen moss.

When I reached our small cabin on the hill overlooking the creek, I stopped and carefully surveyed the brushy flat where I had killed the moose. No sign of the wolves. I went on down into the creek bottom to the meat cache. Sure enough, the wolves had found it, and their tracks were all around in the fresh snow. One of them had climbed on the brush pile and pulled away a few of the boughs. But whether they had been spooked by our coming behind them or had found the cache unnatural and therefore dangerous, they did not touch the meat. All three of them had left the cache and gone up the creek toward Shamrock divide. That afternoon and the next morning we dragged the heavy quarters to the hill behind the cabin, and hung them high from a rack between two spruce trees. Neither wolf nor lynx nor anything else bothered the meat that winter.

And once on a cool and overcast September afternoon when we had gone to the river to check the salmon net, we heard what might have been a short cry, and saw a brownish wolf loping upriver on the dry sandbars.

There was no ravenous wolf pack in full tongue chasing the dogsled homeward, nor a ring of bright and famished eyes waiting beyond the bivouac fire to be kept at bay by a blazing brand flung now and then into the darkness; nor from the darkness yelps and whimpers and the smell of singed fur—or so a story went that I read once many years ago.

But listen. One winter night I was awakened by something—a board in the house wall cracking in the frost. I got out of bed, went to the door, and looked out the window to the cleared slope beyond the yard. Deep snow and bright moonlight lay on the hillside. I saw four dark shapes there, moving slowly uphill toward the timber. My field glasses were hanging from a nail close to the door; I quickly reached for them and put them up to my eyes. In that bright light I saw the wolves clearly—three of them grey and white, and one nearly black in the lead.

They did not stay long in the open; the timber was close, and they were soon absorbed in its shadows. But one of them paused for a moment and looked down toward the cabin, arrested by the rattling of a chain as one of our dogs came out of his shelter to look. Although it stood half in the shadow of the birches, I could see clearly the intent wolf face, its eyes and small ears, and the grey coat of fur standing thickly in the mottled moonlight. And then it too was gone. I opened the door and stood briefly in the cold on the open porch. But there was not a sound in that moonlit stillness.

The next morning when it was light I walked up the hill and found their tracks in the snow. They had come up from the river, crossed the road not far from our cabin, and gone up through the woods toward Banner Creek. The snow was loose and dry, and the wolves had plowed through it, each one leaving a shallow trough behind him. It was only in the hard snow by the roadside that I found a pair of firm, clear prints, and knew without question that they had indeed been wolves and not the phantoms of sleep.

Once before on a bright spring afternoon one of our dogs woofed and pointed its muzzle toward the river. Down there on the glittering, windswept expanse of snow we saw five wolves traveling downriver. I thought at first they might be a family of coyotes, but when I looked with the glasses I saw that they were too large and heavy bodied. At the sound made by our dog, three of them halted and looked up toward the house. It was a long rifle shot even with a scope, four hundred yards or better, and steeply downhill into that sunny glare; I was only briefly tempted to try it. The wolves went on, trotting swiftly over the hard snowcrust, and were soon out of sight around the bluffs. Our four dogs barked and howled, but no answer came from the river.

Something like an answer came one night toward spring a few years later. We were awakened by a sound coming faintly though the walls of the cabin, like a distant singing. We got out of bed, and since it was a mild, clear night we went outdoors and stood in the snow to listen.

Far across the Tanana, a mile or more to the south of us, a group of wolves was singing. I call it singing, not howling, for that is what it was like. We could distinguish three, perhaps four voices—wavering, ascending in pitch, each one following on the other, until they all broke off in a confused chorus. Their voices sank into distant echoes on the frozen river, and began again. A light and uncertain wind was blowing out there, and the sound grew and faded as the air brought it toward us or carried it away southward. It might have come across a thousand years of ice and wind-packed snow, traveling as the light of stars from a source no longer there.

The singing was brief, a few short minutes. Chilled by the night air, we turned to go back indoors. Night, a breezy darkness, claimed the icebound river, and the only sound was the distant throb of a diesel rig on the road toward Fairbanks.

Lost

NOW AND THEN PEOPLE DISAPPEAR in the Far North and are never heard from again. For various reasons: they are lost, drowned, or frozen to death. It was common enough in early days when so many were traveling the country on foot and by water and often alone. Yet in recent memory whole planeloads of people have dropped out of sight, the fuselage with its frozen bodies found years later in a snowdrift on a remote mountainside.

I remember one spring morning when a group of men came down the road at Richardson. We watched them as they searched the roadside thickets and probed the snowdrifts with poles. They were looking for an old woman who had left her house near Big Delta a few evenings before, and had not come back. Family and neighbors thought she may have walked in her half-sleep into the nearby river, to be swept away under the ice. But they couldn't be sure. They went on down the road, a scattered troop of brown and grey soon lost to view in the cold sunlight.

And there was the fellow who disappeared from his Quartz Lake trapline a few winters back. Said to be a little strange in his head and mistrustful of people, he had been long absent in the bush when a search was begun by his brother and the police. Although the country was flown over and searched for weeks, he too was never found alive. But two or three years later someone hunting in the backcountry came upon a pair of leg bones and some scraps of blue wool cloth with metal buttons. Most of the bones had been carried off by animals, and it was impossible by then to say who he was or what had happened to him.

There are people lost in more ways than one. Like the man named Abrams, active for a while in the Birch Lake area many years ago. Despondent over something or other, he walked away from camp one late winter day and did not come back. No one followed him then, but he was found eventually in an old cabin up on one of the Salcha River tributaries, dead. He had cut both his wrists, and bled to death lying in a makeshift bunk.

I was told once of the end of a man whose name will have to be Hanson, since I cannot remember his real name. He drove mail by dogsled in an early day, out of Fairbanks and up the Tanana beyond Big Delta. It was sixty below zero one January day when he stopped at McCarty Station on his way upriver. He was urged not to continue, but to stay at the roadhouse for a day or so and wait for a promised break in the weather. An experienced man, he decided to go on. He was well dressed for it, and carried a good robe on his sled. But his dogs whined in the foggy, windless cold, and would rather have stayed.

A few days later his dogs came back, dragging the sled behind them, but without Hanson. The cold had broken by then, and men went out, following the sled trail back upriver. Some thirty miles on they found Hanson crouched beside a stack of driftwood, his arms folded on his chest, and his head down. He did not move or speak when they walked up on him. One of the men touched him, and found that they had been calling to a stone. At his feet were the charred makings of a fire that had never caught.

Although I have never been lost in the woods, I have known that momentary confusion when a strange trail divided or thinned out before me, and I have stopped there on a hillside in the wind-matted buckbrush and willows, wondering which of the many possible roads I ought to take. I have come home late through the woods at night and missed my trail underfoot, to stand undecided, listening for something in the darkness: the wind moving aloft in the trees, the sound of a dry leaf skittering over the snowcrust, or the sudden crashing of an animal disturbed.

Fred Campbell told me once of being shut in by fog on Buckeye Dome one fall day, a fog so thick he could not see the ground at his feet. He lost all sense of place and time, and wandered that day in an endless and insubstantial whiteness. It seemed to him at times that he was not walking on earth, but was stranded in a still cloud, far from anything he could touch or know. Toward evening the sun burned a hole in the mist, and he found his way down into familiar woods again.

That lostness and sinking of things, so close to the ordinariness of our lives. I was mending my salmon net one summer afternoon, leaning over the side of my boat in a broad eddy near the mouth of Tenderfoot. I had drawn the net partway over the gunwale to work on it, when a strong surge in the current pulled the meshes from my hand. As I reached down to grasp the net again I somehow lost hold of my knife, and watched half-sickened as it slipped from my hand and sank out of sight in the restless, seething water.

Poling upriver in the fall, maneuvering the nose of my boat through the slack, freezing water; or wading over stones and gravel in the shallow current, while the boat tugged behind me at the end of a doubled rope; or again, as I floated down on the turbulent summer water, swinging my oars in response to the drift-piles looming swiftly ahead: how easily I might be spilled and swept under, my boat to be found one day lodged in driftwood, an oar washed up on the sand, and myself a sack weighted with silt, turning in an eddy.

A drowsy, half-wakeful menace waits for us in the quietness of this world. I have felt it near me while kneeling in the snow, minding a trap on a ridge many miles from home. There, in the cold that gripped my face, in the low, blue light failing around me, and the short day ending, in those familiar and friendly shadows, I was suddenly aware of something that did not care if I lived. Or, as it may be, running the river ice in midwinter: under the sled runners a sudden cracking and buckling that scared the dogs and sent my heart racing. How swiftly the solid bottom of one's life can go.

Disappearances, apparitions; few clues, or none at all. Mostly it isn't murder, a punishable crime—the people just vanish. They go away, in sorrow, in pain, in mute astonishment, as of something decided forever. But sometimes you can't be sure, and a thing will happen that remains so unresolved, so strange, that someone will think of it years later; and he will sit there in the dusk and silence, staring out the window at another world.

The Sack of Bones

I HEARD THIS STORY FROM Hans Seppala late one summer evening. We were sitting in his cabin at Shaw Creek, drinking coffee, smoking, and talking. A few mosquitoes sailed about the room, half-stunned by the smoke. Out the open door of the cabin, in the midnight dusk, we could hear the creek flowing by, but with hardly a sound in its slow, brown current. The landscape held that unusual quiet, when for an hour or so, before the sun lights up the hills again, the life of the arctic summer is stilled, and few birds sing.

Hans had his fund of stories, which he told with particular emphasis in his own kind of English, generous with obscenities, and half formed on the syntax of his native Finn. Like most of the old people I knew, he told many of the same stories over and over, hardly changing the details, and laughing gleefully in the same places. Most of his stories were about people we both knew, or someone who had once lived in the area but was now gone. Some figure of whom he might say something playful or outrageous. But this story was different; he told it once, and I never heard it again.

One fall back in the 1930s, a man named Martin came to trap on Shaw Creek flats, ten miles east of Richardson. He found a vacant cabin a few miles up the creek, and moved into it with his axe, his traps, and what few other things he owned. Snow came, and he was soon active, running some of the old, brushed-in trails that went far back in the flats and into the hills rising north and west.

97

Now it happened that Fred Campbell and Emory Hershberger had a trapping partnership at the time, and they included Shaw Creek in their territory, as most people knew. When they got wind of Martin in the area they were a little put out. They went to see him one day early in November, and explained that they were first on the ground, and how would it be if he went somewhere else. No one who meant well intruded on another's trapline as he was doing. But Martin was a tough and ornery man, and would not listen. It did not matter to him that they had trapped there before; no one owned that land, and he had as much right to be there as anyone. They could go to hell.

There was an angry exchange between them, some hard words were spoken. Campbell and Hersh left, Campbell muttering and Hersh tight lipped. The more they thought about Martin the angrier they got. They were ready men, each of them prone to go his own road and say nothing. But one of them was heard to say afterwards that they would take care of Martin in their own way: "Dead men tell no tales."

The following spring an acquaintance of Martin's named Wade came down from Fairbanks to see him. He walked the hard-packed snowshoe trail in from the road. It was early in a March evening; the cold had broken, and a warm wind was blowing through the spruce forest.

Wade found the cabin door open when he arrived at Martin's camp. No one seemed to be at home. From a rusty stovepipe stuck at an angle through the sod roof, smoke drifted down and thinned among the trees. He went into the cabin and looked around. Martin was not a particularly clean man; the cabin smelled of skins, of old and unwashed clothing, and smoke. Four or five fox and lynx pelts were drying on stretchers in a corner away from the heat. A supper of beans and meat lay on the table, half-eaten, and the stove was still warm with its smoldering wood.

Searching around the camp area in the fading light, Wade could find no immediate trace of Martin, but foot-trails going off into the snow-filled woods in several directions. He called once or twice, but got no answer.

He waited until it was nearly dark, then wrote a note and left it on the table. He closed the cabin door, and walked back through the dim woods to the road. He casually asked at the house of some people living nearby on the river if anyone had seen Martin lately. No one had, but no one thought much of that at the time.

The weeks went by. The sun climbed higher; snow came again, and melted, and still Martin had not been seen. Another visitor to his cabin found Wade's note on the table, and nothing apparently changed. The word went around between Richardson and Delta. A search was begun in the frozen swamps along Shaw Creek, and in the woods around Martin's camp. No clues were found.

Summer came, the ice went out of Shaw Creek with a roar one midnight, and soon after that the Tanana ice moved downriver. The small cabin in the spruce flats was closed up by a marshal from Fairbanks, and the man named Martin was never seen again.

Hans stopped talking. He reached for his papers and tobacco, and began rolling another cigarette.

"Did you know Martin yourself?" I asked him.

"Vell, I know him a little, but I wasn't around the Shaw Creek very much in them days."

He licked the paper, smoothed it, and struck a match. Staring out the window, he drew on the cigarette, and sent a cloud of smoke into the dusky room.

"So, anyvay . . ." And he went on with his story.

Two years went by, and Martin had almost been forgotten. Late in a spring evening Hans came across the Tanana ice with his dogs, a few miles downriver from the mouth of Shaw Creek. It was nearly breakup time, warm in the day, but piercing cold at night. Water had flowed over the ice in places, and frozen again in a thin, perilous sheet. Coming late in the near darkness, Hans and his dogs broke through the ice into knee-deep water.

Steaming and cursing, he pulled himself, his dogs and sled,

onto firm ice. Then, tangled and wet, they ran for a nearby island. There Hans built a fire from driftwood, and set up camp to dry out.

It froze hard that night; the new ice cracked and whistled, and the stars glittered in the brief spring darkness. Hans lay wrapped in his damp bedroll, hardly able to sleep for the cold.

The next morning he was up early; it had been a cold and exposed emergency camp, and he was eager to be on his way home. Snow had blown away from the island in the winter gales, and what remained of it lay packed in thin, hard drifts, snow and ice and sand mixed together. Here and there, stones, pieces of driftwood, small willows, and clumps of stiff grass stood out from the wind-packed waste.

"So, I getting up that morning, still half wet. Clothes, they frozen. The dogs, they hungry, but I got nothing to feed them. I look for a little dry wood to make a fire and have a cup of coffee. And then, by God, I find something in the driftwood!"

Wedged partway into a large pile of driftwood was an odd bundle of canvas and poles wrapped 'round with heavy wire. Curious now, Hans pulled at the bundle and saw something that looked like the rounded and bleached joint-end of a bone sticking out from the rotted fabric. He looked closer, pulled at the bone, and saw that another came with it.

"What the Jesus Christ is this? I say to meself. I look at them bones; they not the moose bones, they not heavy enough. I hold one up to my leg, and another one to my arm. And by God, they look like the human bones!"

The bundle was half filled with frozen sand and small stones. Searching in it as well as he could, Hans found other pieces of bone: a rib, and an arm bone. What looked like a shoulder blade was showing from the frozen debris packed into the bundle. But there was no skull.

The bundle would not come free of the frozen driftwood, and when he pulled at it the canvas tore. But Hans could see that two bleached poles ran either side the length of it. And he saw that it might have been made as a kind of stretcher, the whole thing fastened together with some pieces of common telegraph wire, wound and twisted tightly on the poles.

Hans realized that he had found something important, but he was not sure what it was. There was nothing to identify a human body, other than the few bones and the way it was all put together. He stopped there, unsure of what to do. The sun was climbing, he wanted to have his coffee and be on his way. He thought of chopping the bundle free of the wood and ice, and taking it on his sled. But that would take time, and his sled was already full. He decided to leave the bundle where it was, and tell someone at Richardson what he had found.

He replaced the bones in the sack more or less as he had found them. He gathered wood, made a small fire, and drank his coffee. He packed his sled, laid out the stiff harness, and then with the dogs yelping and pulling hard for home, he struck out over the ice toward Richardson.

Much later in the day, when he had unloaded his sled and fed his dogs, Hans walked to the roadhouse. Drinking his first beer in many weeks, he talked to Knute Johanson, who in his aging, unbusinesslike, and bad-tempered way, still kept the trade going. Hans told him what he had found.

Knute immediately showed interest. "Yah!" he exclaimed. "By God, Hans, you should have brought one of the bones back with you! What did dey look like?"

And Hans told him, in what detail he could, while Knute peered at him, his narrow eyes screwed up in his homely face. In both their minds by now was the disappearance of Martin some years before. Knute, suspicious as always, was already convinced that they *were* Martin's bones, though how they got there on that island neither he nor Hans was prepared to say.

They talked, and the questions came as they did so. Had anyone else disappeared in the past three or four years? What else could that sack of bones be? And why would anyone truss up a sack of animal bones that way?

Hans was to return across river in a day or so, and when he did he would bring back the entire bundle on his sled. That was agreed. No, perhaps it would be better to bring back one of the bones, rather than disturb the whole thing. But mark the island for sure, so we can find it again. And you'd better go soon, the river will begin to open in a few days if the sunlight holds.

Like all young rivers, the Tanana does strange and unpredictable things. Its channels shift from summer to summer, and each high water changes the cold, grey face of the riverbed. One year a small island will stand there in midchannel, shaggy with its willows and young cottonwoods seeded by the wind, or planted there by what the water brings down. And the next year that island is gone, its young growth toppled and swept under by the summer flood. Or the spring ice builds to make a dam; the river backs up and floods the countryside. Ice floes float into town, cabins come loose from their moorings. The ice dam breaks, and the river falls, running easily with its chunks of rotten ice, dead carcasses, lost boats, and trash.

Hans stayed at Richardson one day too long, visiting and drinking, cutting wood and getting ready for the summer. On an evening before he was to go back across the river, a channel opened up on the north side. There was no way across; his boat was at Clear Creek, several miles off on the far side of the river. He would have to wait. Nearly three weeks went by before he caught a ride upriver with a man going to Clear Creek for the early summer fishing.

"So, we going up the river in that big powerboat. The river running pretty swift, lots of ice and plenty of driftwood coming down. I watch for that island, and I think I see him. So when I come back down the river in my own boat, I stop there, and I look. It look to me like the same place, but I can't be sure."

Part of the island seemed to be as he remembered it when it was locked in ice, but the big raft of driftwood with its rotting sack of bones was gone. Where it might have been, some young cottonwoods leaned out over the water, their roots exposed in the shallow soil cut away by the current.

"Oh, that Hans!" said Sandra, the cook at Richardson, some time later. "It was probably something he dreamed up while he was drunk. You can't believe what he says."

And who could say, really, what it had been? It might have been Martin. And it was easy enough to imagine the circumstances, the accumulating resentment that came to a decision: Martin surprised one afternoon by two others who called him out of his cabin, and killed him with a gun or an axe. They carried him away, trussed his body in a sack weighted with stones, and sank him in an open channel late at night. It wouldn't have been hard to do, there were few people along the river in those days. But no one would ever know for sure; no one else was talking, and the Tanana kept its secrets.

We sat there thinking about this strange event, the coffee gone cold in our cups. Morning brightened in the forest beyond Hans's clearing, a fine mist came off the water of Shaw Creek. Hans turned from the window. He opened the stove door and began poking at the few live coals. Then he spoke again.

"People think I just telling the big story, but I know what I saw. And to this day I still believe that they be the Martin's bones."

He turned, and looked at me sharply and strangely through the steel rims of his spectacles.

Mudding Up

A CLEAR AFTERNOON IN MID-SEPTEMBER 1947. You will know the kind of day I mean: a warm, tawny light over the hills, the sky is flawless in its clarity, and already in the windless air leaves drift down from the birches and aspens.

In the broad field above the river bluff the hay stubble and the uncut grasses are washed to a dry, translucent yellow. Here and there a few stalks of fireweed and dock stand rusty and strong; their feathery seed-bolls are tattered, blown empty in a late-August wind.

A quietness over the land. The noise of summer, of high water and road traffic, of mating birds and foraging insects, has mysteriously vanished. One braided channel of the river is only a stone's throw from the edge of the field; yet near as it is, the shallow restlessness of that water over stones and gravel is somehow diminished and distant.

A day when a shout, an axe stroke, or the single cry of a raven, rings clear and remote. The humming of a few late wasps searching the browned marigolds, the drone of a bumblebee, surging and resting, fills the hollow of all creation.

Allison and I are mudding up the walls in the old Richardson stable, making it tight for the winter. We have been at work three days, and this is the last.

Each afternoon we have walked across the road from the roadhouse, to find our tools laid aside late on the previous day. It has been some years now since horses were stabled here. The low, big-timbered building has sunk down in the sod, the original chinking has fallen away, leaving here and there a gap for wind and frost. But the metaled roof is sound, the stalls are still in place, and the earthen floor is deep in old, rotted hay and long-trampled manure. This fall Allison has turned the stable into a chicken house, and he wants his hens to be warm in the long dark that is coming.

According to age and agility we have divided the work as we have moved ever higher up the grey, weather-cracked wall. I stand now on a rung of the wooden ladder, working with trowel and mortarboard. Allison is on the ground below, mixing the peaty soil with water into a square-sided five-gallon tin opened lengthwise to make a shallow trough. With a practiced stroke he stirs the brown mud-mortar back and forth with a stump of a hoe.

"Was you in the war?" Allison stopped in his mud-mixing for a moment, and glanced up at me out of the shadow he stood in.

"Oh, sure," I answered him, "three years in the navy in the Pacific."

"See much action?" He squinted up at me from under the brim of his cap.

"Oh, yeah, enough—more than enough."

I am none too talkative at best, and on that calm afternoon, a long way from the absurdities of global politics, of military rank and imposed duties, the Pacific War not long past was maybe the last thing I wanted to talk about. But not to be rude, I added, "Mostly, you know, it was just boring—a lot of waiting around for something to happen."

Allison resumed his digging and stirring. "Well," he said, after a short while, "I guess I missed all that."

"How about the first war?"

"Missed that, too," came the answer.

"Just as well," I said, "either way, it wasn't a lot of fun."

But for a moment or two I was back in the war, at sea, standing watch, earphones clamped to my head, scanning a radar screen for a strange flare, a hostile blip, and between watches and battle alerts waiting for the whole thing to end.

And then, not long after the war, I was back in school, standing before an easel, or sitting at a drawing board, trying to fix in form, line, and color something of a world I had yet to understand any part of.

And briefly I was with a girl I had left behind on coming to Alaska. I could see us now, distant and caught in a cold, slant light, coming out of the city library on a winter afternoon. We were on our way to her house, and each of us carried an armload of books. We were talking together and looking forward to an evening of reading and study.

And all of that passed through my mind and was gone. I came back to this present moment, and to the thing before me, to a simple task of repair I could take pleasure in learning to do. And to whatever was part of that: the glint of mica in the sandy clay soil, the ragged peat moss sticking in the log seams; to nothing more than the split and knotted, weather-greyed wood of the wall in front of me. I saw my hand on the trowel, and the wet, brown mud heaped on the board I held; and below me by the stable wall, Allison's broad and ruddy face in a stray shaft of light. I heard the soft scrape and slop of the water and earth he stirred back and forth in the gleaming tin trough.

As concentrated as I was on the moment, savoring every detail, did I sense that this quiet, rural world of Richardson, with its few surviving people and its old-fashioned implements, remote and settled on a stretch of gravel road, was vanishing even as I came to know it? It may have been that in some hidden part of myself I knew this, knew that I in some way was a part of the change taking place. But for now there was this moment, this day, and the promise of others to come: a vague, but tangible dream realizing itself in the cool, diminishing light of a first fall.

Time passes. The work goes quietly; my mind drifts on ahead by days and weeks. It is afternoon once more; the veiled sun lies much lower in the south, spending its cold, grey light over the river and the fields. A light snow now lies on the ground, no more than an inch over the frost-shattered stubble of grass.

Allison and I have come to the stable to slaughter three of his chickens for the roadhouse kitchen. As we cross the road and head for the door of the stable, Allison, talking half to himself, remarks that the hour is right, and the hens will be settling to sleep in the early dusk and chill of this brief autumn day.

We quietly enter the stable, sliding back the wooden bolt in the heavy plank door. In the hay-scented, semigloom of the interior we approach the hens who are roosting on beams in the old horse stalls. We stand still for a moment as from the shadowy space above comes a subdued clucking and shifting of feathered bodies. Allison reaches up with his gloved hand, takes one hen by its legs, pulls it from its perch, and hands it to me. He does this surely, and with no loss of motion.

We leave the stable as quietly as we came, taking care not to alarm the rest of the small flock. The one rust red hen hangs tense and compact from my hand, the head with its pink comb turning from side to side, the bright, dark eye cocked in wonder. Still half-drugged with sleep, the bird does not cry out or flap its wings.

Outside the stable, in the cold air, we approach a spruce block standing before a pile of cordwood. A double-bitted axe with a worn and polished handle is propped against the block.

With Allison directing me, I hold the chicken firmly and lay its head and neck on the block. Almost inert until now, the hen suddenly tenses and tries to free itself; but I grasp it all the firmer, holding its wings and feet with both hands. Allison takes a short swing with the axe—the head flies off, and at Allison's command I throw the bird away to the ground. We watch as the suddenly headless hen stands up, begins to flap its wings and run swiftly over the wet ground, blood spurting from its severed neck. And then a soft, quivering mound of rusty feathers collapses on the shallow, red-spattered snow.

I have killed more than one wild bird and eaten it, sensed in myself some passing regret at having taken the life of a creature; but this is the first time I have slaughtered a domestic chicken. It is a lesson, as not long ago the mudding of the stable was a lesson. And so, what with the stealth and the axe and the blood, my sensibilities have been awakened in a way they had not been before. During these fifteen minutes or so of concentrated activity, from the opening of the stable door to the swing of the axe, I have watched Allison and myself with a kind of fascinated horror.

We return to the stable for the second bird. And again the head flies off to the sound of the axe in the block, and again the headless bird flaps and runs and falls. On our third visit to the stable we find the hens awake and clucking in alarm, and Allison has some trouble catching one of them by the legs. We succeed, and once more we stand by the bloody block and watch that briefly quickened bundle of rusty feathers subsiding in the snow.

And then that work is done. We leave the axe in the block by the stable. Carrying the dead hens by their legs, Allison with two and I with one, we walk through dry, standing weeds and cross the graveled road and yard to the kitchen. That evening Allison's wife, Babe, will draw and pluck the birds. There will be roast and fried chicken for the table, chicken soup for the house, and one bird sent to a friend in town.

Already in the field behind us it is dusk and colder. Soon it will be night.

Now in the shadow of the stable wall the air took on a deeper chill. Allison looked up from where he was standing over his trough, his face ruddy with work and the cold. With that one startling blue eye of his he sent a keen and searching glance over the upper wall, and remarked that our job was nearly done.

I pushed the last of the mud on my board into the moss-chinked seam of the log I was working on. Deliberately I smoothed the cold mud, working it into the gap with the blade of my trowel. When I had finished, I leaned back away from the ladder to look, and felt a small rush of satisfaction. The log seams looked neat with their brown, drying mud-streaks. Rough-fashioned though it was, the stable would be tight and warm for the winter.

With my board and trowel I climbed back down the ladder to the ground. While Allison emptied his trough and cleaned his shovel and hoe, I scraped the mortarboard, knocked it to free one last, clinging lump, and wiped the trowel on the dry grass stubble at my feet. As we had done on the previous day, and the day before that, we set our tools aside under the shelter of the stable wall.

Evening was coming on. Now that the afternoon work was over, I was conscious that my hands were cold, that my entire body was chilled from standing so long on the ladder. I took off the damp gloves I had been wearing, and shoved my hands into the pockets of my jacket. To judge from a sudden sharpness in the air, there would be frost that night.

As we walked back toward the roadhouse, I replied to something Allison had said by way of thanking me for the help I had given him. It was nothing, I said; I had learned something in exchange.

We stopped for a moment by the roadside. A truck pounded by, big and single, raising a cold cloud of dust that slowly drifted away in the windless air. In the following quiet, Allison and I agreed that in a day or two I would return to help him saw up some firewood. Behind us, to one side of the stable, a long rough pile of spruce timbers lay in the grass; in the roadhouse yard another cord or two, loosely stacked, waited for the big, gas-powered saw.

I turned from Allison at the edge of the road. I would not join them for supper that evening; I had chores of my own to do at home. We said good-bye, and while there was still light in the woods I began walking the long stretch of road through the flat toward a familiar hill that rose before me, a high, yellow mass still sunlit on its crest.

The early evening was quiet and chill. No birdsong came from the woods to either side of the road. I could hear the river, subdued and distant through the trees; heard, too, in the brief time it took me to cross, the calm flow of water in Banner Creek under the tarred plank bridge. The only other sound was the crunching of my boots in the loose gravel of the roadside.

From somewhere now I caught the scent of wood smoke on the evening air. Someone I had yet to meet was cooking supper off there in the woods away from the road. The thought reminded me that I was hungry, that I had not eaten since noon. It would be close to seven o'clock, I guessed. I had no watch, but I was learning to read the light, coming low now through a slot in the hills downriver.

No traffic on the road, no wheels, no dust. I walked along, one foot before the other, alone on the gravelly, turning roadbed. As I walked, I looked often into the dim woods on either side of the road. I looked for nothing in particular, but only to silently name the trees, to read the shadows under the birches and aspens. I was thinking of supper, of wood and water, of things far and near that came and went in my mind.

At the high point of the bluff, where the road began a slow curve and descent, I stopped to look out over the river in the growing dusk. Light lay over the water, on the islands and the hills in the distance, so pervasive and steeped in its yellowness, it was hard to tell if that light came from the evening sky or welled up from somewhere in the autumn earth itself.

I listened to the pebbly sound of the river falling through diminished channels below me. And for a long moment I felt myself a part of that landscape with its shaggy, black islands and pale sandbars, one with the coppery gleam of water coiling and darkening, the distant country of night.

I turned and walked on. Soon the homestead hill and the deep shadow of the creek bottom came into view. I crossed the road, began to climb toward the small, unlighted house on a cleared shelf of the hillside.

And evening followed.

Dusk

ONE AUGUST NIGHT, ON THE TRAIL BACK from McCoy Creek, Fred Campbell and I stopped to rest. The fall darkness was coming on, and we had been walking for the past hour in a very dim twilight. As we stood for a moment, hunched under our packs and leaning on our walking sticks, we heard overhead in the windless quiet of the evening a small explosive sound, a snap or a chirp, like nothing I had heard before.

"What was that?" I asked.

"Flying squirrel, I think."

Maybe once or twice afterwards in my night journeys home through the woods I heard a sound like that—a dry, sharp chirp in the trees above me, though I could see nothing near me in the darkness. It was a sound related to the creaking of tree limbs rubbed together in the wind, a sound that belonged to the night.

But late one winter a flying squirrel came to the bird feeder set on a shelf by the house. It may have been attracted by the window light, or had at dusk observed the birds coming and going. Once it had discovered the feeder, the squirrel came at dusk or after dark, seldom by day, to feed on the cornmeal, bread scraps, suet, and seed put out for the winter chickadees and woodpeckers.

We always knew when the squirrel arrived by the sudden "thump" of its landing on the feeder roof. By light of the one lamp set indoors by the window, we watched it hunched in the cold, nibbling and alert: a compact, delicately formed creature, its rich fur grizzled grey and brown, a pale underbelly, and with the large dark eyes of a nocturnal animal. It soon became familiar enough to allow one of us to approach the feeder closely and put out more food. The squirrel barely paused in its munching of seeds, its dark eyes shining in the subdued glare of a flashlight.

One evening, just after sunset, when the flying squirrel had been at the house for a short time, I watched it leave the feeder. It sprang to the trunk of the large aspen that grew beside the house, climbed quickly to the top, and launched itself into the air toward a nearby birch. I saw it sail without difficulty to a landing on the lower trunk of the birch; it rapidly climbed that tree, from which it again launched itself into the forest.

Thinking later on that skilled and effortless flight in the dusk, I recalled how once years before I had in fun shaken a red squirrel from a tree to amuse the dogs. The squirrel was high in a slender willow, and there were no other trees of size close enough for it to jump to. As my shaking increased and the willow swayed back and forth, the squirrel, braced in the topmost branches, suddenly launched into the air. I saw it come down in a kind of slow-motion descent, its four legs outspread and tail held stiff and straight with the long hairs flattened; it seemed to float to the ground. It fell with a soft thump on the dry autumn sod not far from where I stood, having fallen a distance of more than thirty feet. It lay still for a moment; then, recovered from the shock of its landing, and before the dogs could grab it, it ran to the trunk of a larger tree nearby and climbed to safety.

In that brief exhibition of daring and skill I saw how a night-feeding squirrel might, given sufficient time, say a million years or so, stretch the loose skin of its body and develop that sailing skill to perfection.

Later in the spring a second flying squirrel came to the feeder, and there were two of them. They remained through the spring and well into the summer, and it began to look as if we might have them as permanent residents on the homestead. But one day we returned from a camping trip to find one of the squirrels floating face down in a rain barrel. The barrel stood near the southwest corner of the house, a few feet from the bird feeder; at the time the barrel was somewhat more than half filled with water. Somehow the squirrel had fallen in and had been unable to climb out. Afterwards I put a screen over the barrel, but it was too late. The remaining squirrel never returned to the feeder.

And then the following winter a flying squirrel was found dead at the roadhouse. A door to one of the sheds had been left open, and the squirrel had apparently been attracted to a sack of dog food that was stored there. The door was then closed and the squirrel, unable to get out, had frozen. It was curled up on a shelf in a hard little ball, a furry knot of frozen energy.

Knowing that I was an occasional trapper, the owner of the roadhouse asked me to skin the squirrel for him so that he could hang it on the wall of his bar as part of his fur collection.

I took the small, stiff animal home, so small that it fitted easily into the pocket of my parka. I thawed it out and carefully skinned it. After some trial, I fashioned a thin, flat board on which to stretch the delicate pelt. It stretched out more or less square, about seven by eight inches, its thin flying membrane of skin and hair attached like a cape or a sail between the tiny, clawed forefeet and hind feet. The dry pelt with its soft, rich fur made a pleasing pattern of contrasting brown and cream color edged with black.

Years ago at Richardson a hungry fox came to feed at the roadhouse. It came by night, over the snow, with its red fur and thick tail brush tipped with black and white hairs; and shyly, sometimes with a growl of mistrust, it gripped the meaty bone held out to it, and ran away into the darkness.

On Thanksgiving night a number of people from the neighborhood and from along the highway were gathered at the roadhouse to eat and drink, to sing and dance. The fox came that evening, got its ration, and was seen by all. Later, in a brief moment of quiet, a car was heard to stop on the road outside. Then, above the renewed noise of the music and talk, something like a muffled gunshot was heard, and the car drove on. Someone from the gathering went outdoors to investigate, and found a fresh pool of blood freezing in the roadside snow.

And again, on a Christmas night, we neighbors were gathered at the roadhouse. The snowfall that winter was deep against the outside wall, heaped under the eaves nearly to the level of the windowsill. It was a time of scarcity in the woods, when rabbits were few and the carnivores were hard pressed to make a living.

During the course of the evening someone called out to the rest of the company, and we looked up from the bar to a window set high in the wall. A full-grown coyote stood there in the houselight, looking down into the room. Gaunt and famished-looking in its grizzled, tawny fur, it stood for that moment framed in the window like a very accurate painting. The intense yellow eyes stared briefly into the light and the sudden quiet of the room. Then, realizing that it had been discovered, the grey ghost form turned and vanished.

An old friend and neighbor who lived on the far side of Birch Lake, some ten miles west of Richardson, for several years kept a pet woodchuck. It had been given to him when it was very young by a member of a survey crew who had found it strayed from its home burrow. Fed and nurtured, the animal grew fat and tame, tolerated by the one other member of the household, an aging husky.

Each fall, when the birch leaves had blown to the ground and the lake water began to freeze along the shoreline; when the first flurry of snow came drifting across the cold, dark lake, the woodchuck retreated to a den it had dug under a corner of the woodshed. Snow soon covered the entrance, and the woodchuck did not emerge until late in the following spring. It appeared then, blinking at the strong light, to sit in the sun and groom its thick, grizzled brown fur. And once more at home in the summer light, it moved about the yard in its chubby body, to search the patches of bare ground for fresh shoots and summer greens.

And early each summer, when its mating season arrived, the woodchuck took up a post on the chopping block or on top of the doghouse. Erect and watchful, it chattered and whistled, sending a piercing note over the meadow and into the nearby woods. But however long it sat and waited and whistled, no mate ever appeared. The woodchuck went into hibernation in a kind of tooth-muttering rage, to try again the following summer.

As it grew older, it became surly and aggressive, possessive of what it regarded as its home territory—the yard, the woodshed, and the house—and strongly protective of its mixed human and canine family. With growing fierceness it attacked any stranger to the homestead, growling, clicking its big front teeth together in a loud and menacing way, and often chasing an unwary visitor into the house. To curb the creature, my friend sometimes found it necessary to corner it with a broom and drive it into the wire mink cage he kept handy. Once locked in, the woodchuck would rattle and rock and snarl and bite the wire, working itself into a greater rage, before it calmed down and went to sleep.

Finally, with regret, one day in late summer he herded the woodchuck into its cage. He took it by boat across the lake, and then by car to a wooded place several miles from home where he turned it loose. It never found its way back to Birch Lake. Its burly, chattering little presence was missed from time to time. We never knew if it survived alone in the country or, whether, foraging for itself on a dry and sunny slope, it finally found a mate and some late fulfillment of its baffled nature.

Early in my summer work at Richardson, while I was clearing trees on the hillside above the homestead yard, I heard a whimpering sound in the woods, a sound soulful and pathetic, like an abandoned baby crying. It seemed to come from a source close to the earth and not far from me, and yet I could not determine its location. I wondered if there was not a young bear close by whimpering for its mother, and I gazed apprehensively into the gloomy summer woods.

Sometime later, while visiting Fred Campbell, I described the sound and asked him what he thought it might be. He considered for a moment, then smiled and looked at me in that understanding, slightly superior way of his, and said that it was probably a porcupine looking for a mate. "They make that sound about this time of year, wandering in the woods. Seems like it can come from anywhere, and right out of the ground. I'll swear, you can look hard for the critter and not find it!"

Years later, on an early summer afternoon, I was walking back to the house from the mailbox when I again heard that plaintive, whimpering sound from somewhere on the dry hillside across the creek and somewhat below me. I decided then that I would attempt to call the animal to me and know for certain what it was.

I climbed down from the high shoulder of the road and crouched in a small cleared space at the edge of the alder brush. Putting my hands to my mouth, I began to call, imitating as well as I could that strange, intermittent crying. And very soon it seemed to me that the animal responded, that we were in communication.

When, in an interval of quiet, no cry came from the woods, I called, and once again, came a response. And soon I heard the sound of something scraping along through the brush, slowly and clumsily crushing last year's leaves under its feet. It stopped, then came on when I again imitated that plaintive crying.

And presently the grass and brush parted, and a large porcupine shoved its black nose into the open and stopped in front of me. It rose on its back legs and stood before me, no more than three feet away. It turned its head to one side so that one dark, unblinking eye regarded me suspiciously.

I kept absolutely still before that nearly blind, questioning gaze, and watched the blunt, black nose working in the air. The porcupine hesitated and leaned toward me as if it might come closer. I felt that with a little more encouragement it might have climbed into my lap, so close was it. But no. The mixed odors of the summer afternoon, combined and sorted by the black, twitching nostrils, found their way into the recesses of the small brain.

The porcupine slowly dropped to the ground and turned to go. It hesitated, half-turned toward me, as if reluctant to give up the promise in the answering voice it had come to. But clearly something was not quite right about my khaki figure crouched there in the sunlight, something alien in the steady gaze that was fastened upon it. The porcupine pulled its yellowish, brindled weight into the woods once more. I heard the small crashing of leaves as it retreated, voiceless and betrayed.

On an October afternoon I was fishing in a channel of the Tanana River. The water was clear, with a small amount of drift ice running in the current. I stood on a sandbar not far from the wooded shoreline, working carefully with a pole and gaffhook; beside me on the snowy sandbar lay a number of red-skinned salmon.

As I stood there, paying close attention to the water and occasionally hooking a salmon, I thought I heard above the sound of the water and ice a scratching noise, and I felt that I was not alone. I turned around and looked up into the woods behind me. The sunlight was grey, diffused by clouds that late afternoon, but I could see in the shadows at the edge of the woods a large fallen poplar stretched out a few feet above the ground. And on top of the fallen tree a large lynx crouched. Its eyes were closed, and slowly and deliberately it was raking the claws of its forefeet in the dry bark of the tree. The animal seemed completely absorbed in what it was doing. I felt that were it not for the sound of the river at my back I could almost hear the big cat purring in a deep, throaty contentment.

The lynx paused in its raking. Its eyes opened, and it turned a wide yellow gaze upon me. There was no alarm in that look, no flash of recognition or fear. We looked at each other for a moment, each of us gazing into some dim shadow of ourselves. And then, not wanting to prolong my stare, as casually as I could I turned back to my fishing. When I looked again, the lynx was gone.

Death Is a Meadowlark

LONG BEFORE I WENT TO LIVE in the woods my awareness of death seemed to have a depth beyond any exact recall. It existed as a memory composed of discontinuous images: a snake crushed on the summer roadway, reeking in the sun—how dull and flattened it was compared to the live snake, supple and glistening, I had seen in the grass a week before. A drowned and bloated frog I had pulled from the bottom of a backyard pool and held in my hand: a wonder—why did it not breathe? A bird in whose decaying nostrils small white worms were coiling. These were the naked things of an uninstructed childhood in which there was little instinctive fear.

And had I not seen as a child the crushed body of a woman sprawled at the city curbing? She had jumped from a window ledge many stories above, and lay concealed by the brown heap of her clothing. Nothing else of her was visible from where I stood, clutched by my mother on a crowded downtown street. There had been the sound of a scream, a sudden rush of air, a glimpse of a spread shape flying down, and the thudding shock of her landing. I was hurried away, and I saw no more.

And there had been also my own near death by drowning late in the first decade of my life. Death had taken the form of a watery green darkness into which I was sinking, slowed and numbed by the depth and cold, while above me the strange, lost sight of sunlight faded from the surface.

It was not then, but a later time, when I was about thirteen. We

118

lived on the edge of uninhabited countryside at the end of a street in suburban California. From our backyard a pathway led uphill into open fields.

One Sunday morning in spring, after the family had returned from church and we had eaten a late breakfast, I went for a long walk alone over the fields. I do not remember what was on my mind then, confused by the unsorted emotions of youth or, as it may have been, delighting in the open sky and the sun on the warm grasses.

The pathway soon merged with a narrow country road. The bare soil in the wheel tracks was damp from the winter rains, and there was an occasional shallow pool of water in a deeper rut. As I came over the crest of the hill I saw something lying at the side of the road just ahead of me. When I came up to it, I saw that it was a rabbit, and that it was dead. Its brown and white fur was torn and its belly ripped open.

I came closer and stopped before it. Just for a moment I stood there looking down at the torn, but still intact animal. The blue bulge of its gut lay half spilled from the body and shone brightly, glazed with blood, in the morning sunlight. A few flies already buzzed around it.

A nameless panic gripped me. I heard the buzzing of the flies and other insects, and somewhere close but out of sight a meadowlark was singing. There was nothing else around, no other sign of man, of animal or bird of prey. Beyond the hillcrest not even a housetop showed above the yellow grasses. I was alone under the sun in an open field with death, unmistakable, physical death.

It was not just that still form lying at the edge of the road, nor the blood that was dried upon its fur; I had seen things like it before. It was something new—an awakening that fastened on the incredible shining blueness of the inside turned outside, the innermost part ripped from its place and spilled into the light where it did not belong. Gazing, fixed before it in the sunlight, I felt, perhaps for the first time, an absolute aloneness. And I who at that age loved solitude, knew that this was death, the loneliest solitude of all.

In terror I began to walk, away from the scene, over the grassy slope of the hill, but looking behind me all the while as if I expected that quiet, mutilated form to rise from the damp ground and follow me. Perhaps I feared that somewhere in that silent, sunny countryside, in the grass, even in the voice of the meadowlark, death itself was waiting.

I do not know what sermon I had half-listened to that morning in church; something that had deepened my mood and prompted my walk—something about mortality, was it, of death and the hereafter, of reward and damnation? I don't remember. Yet somehow I felt deeply that I was guilty, but of what I did not know.

I walked a long way that morning, troubled and confused. I returned over the same path on my way home. As fearful as I had been, both repelled and attracted, I had to see that form of death again. I had to know.

But when I came again to the place in the road, on the rounded hilltop, there was nothing there. I looked around, thinking I had mistaken the location, and that the dead rabbit was somewhere close by. Its absence now was even more alarming. Had I really seen it? But yes, for here in the brown soil at the edge of the grass was a small, darkened spot that appeared to be blood, and near it a little patch of rabbit fur.

I struggled with explanations. Something—hawk or fox—disturbed originally by my coming, had run off and left its victim in the road. And when I had gone, it returned to claim its food.

Still the feeling of dread remained as I walked on toward home. I think now that I told no one of what I had seen, but kept it as a secret, something shared between me, the grass, and the unseen meadowlark. The impression of that morning stayed with me for a long time, and for a while I avoided that part of the road on my walks. When later I crossed the hill at that spot, alone or with friends, I half-expected to see the rabbit again, to have it rise before me from the grass without warning, and with that large, incredibly distended bulge of its stomach, veined with fat, gleaming so brightly blue and green in the sun. But a ghost-image was all I had; a latent emotion charged with mistrust, and a lingering fear.

Transitory in the field, under the sun, slowly disintegrating under blows of the summer rain, an image of the world's stupendous accident. An instant of inexplicable calm, as on the bright, cold winter day I found a redpoll frozen on a snowbank at the entrance to the homestead road. There was nothing to tell me how the bird came to die there. It may have been stunned by the wind gust from a passing car, or it may have fallen asleep while feeding on the blown seeds of the few weed stalks that showed above the snow, and momentarily warming itself in the cold sun. There was not a mark on its body, not a feather disturbed. Under the downy fluff the tiny feet were stiffened; the eyes were half-closed and crystallized; at either side of the nostrils lay a delicate whisker of frost. The rusty crown of its head was bright with color, and the flushed breast seemed almost warm to my touch. But it was absolutely still, the breast and the heart within it joined in a lump of ice. I held the bird for a moment before putting it to rest again in the snow. It seemed to weigh nothing at all.

In that tiny, quenched image of vitality, a bird like a leaf dropped by the wind in passing, I felt something of our common, friable substance—a shared vulnerability grasped once with insight and passion, and then too easily forgotten. Necessarily forgotten, perhaps, for to keep such a thing constantly before one might be intolerable; the identification would wound too deeply.

I see again the worn, chalk white skull of a caribou left behind on the fall tundra many years ago. One half of an antler poked up from the deep moss in which the skull was lying; the moss and the accumulation of old leaves and plant debris had nearly buried the rest of it from view.

When I tilted the skull slightly, I saw that a thin, green mold clung to the bone below the soil line. There had been no trace there for a long time of meat, of marrow or gristle. All else was bleached, chalky, and crumbling: the upper jaw with a few loose molars, the long thin nostril bone, the eye sockets, and the moldering hollows behind the ears. The remaining antler revealed the worn tooth-marks of rodents who in past years, when the skull was still fresh, had gnawed it for the calcium in the bone.

The small lichens and mosses that had taken root upon the skull were breaking down whatever was left of its structure. It seemed to me as I walked away and turned to view it from a little distance, that the skull was like a small vessel, abandoned by captain and crew; rudderless and demasted, it was sinking into the moss and frozen sod. The wet, green sea-life of the tundra washed over the pale wreck in tiny waves year after year, and sooner or later sun, rain, and frost would claim it completely. Farewell.

On a snowy day early in October I was sitting at breakfast alone in the house at Richardson, gloomy with the knowledge that the moose season had closed and I had yet to get my meat for the winter. I had hunted for better than two weeks, all through the cool, dry days of late September, and had seen nothing but tracks. Winter was coming, there was snow on the ground, nearly eight inches of it already, and I knew that in order to find a moose now I would have to go far into the hills for it, and by the time I got it, late in the rut, the meat was sure to be lean and tough.

As I was cleaning up the breakfast pans and dishes, I thought I heard a sound outside, rather like a low grunt, and one of the dogs chained in the yard gave a sharp "woof." I went to the door and looked out. To my astonishment I saw a large bull moose stalking slowly uphill through the snowy garden.

The moose, plainly in view against the white, cleared ground, paused and looked down toward the house and yard. In those few moments of what seemed to be a kind of mutual recognition, it struck me that the moose was not in the best of condition, that perhaps it had been beaten in a fight, or was overtaken by weariness. But no matter—here was my meat, and right in the yard.

I had a rifle at my hand, but at that moment a car went by on the road below the house, driving slowly because of the fresh snowfall. As keenly as I wanted that moose, I feared that it would be seen if I shot it there in plain view and out of season. I waited, and watched the moose climb the open hill and go out of sight over the crest toward the potato patch.

I decided immediately to follow it, to take another way up the hill and head it off, since the moose seemed to be in no hurry. I dressed myself quickly in overshoes, cap, jacket, and gloves, and with the rifle in hand I took off up the hill through the falling snow.

I climbed through the woods, following a trail I had cut the year before. I did not dare to stop for rest, but plowed on, hoping that the snowfall and the laden branches would dampen any sound I was making. In a short time I reached the top of a narrow ridge where the trail began to level off. And there I found the tracks of the moose who had just passed before me. He could not be far ahead. Panting, stumbling at times in the fresh snow, I followed those tracks, determined to catch up with that moose or fall in the snow from trying.

Within a quarter of a mile I came to a place where the trail straightened and I could see some distance ahead of me. Another twenty yards, and I caught up with the moose, now a large brown bulk blurred by the falling snow, standing in the birches. He was stopped in the trail, his head half turned, looking back in my direction.

Trembling from the long climb, I raised the rifle, trying for some kind of shooting rest against the nearest tree. As I was doing this, the moose, alerted now, broke into a trot and began to move swiftly ahead. I had no time for a better shot; he would soon be out of sight, and I was too badly winded from the climb to pursue him any farther. I aimed for a spot just below the tail stump and fired.

At the sound of the shot the moose jumped, ran forward at a faster pace, and stopped. As I approached him, he turned to one side of the trail and stepped slowly into the woods, as if he would think awhile on what had happened. In the one large, dark eye turned toward me I could see a kind of blunted panic and bewilderment. I was ready to shoot again, not knowing if I really had him, when he staggered, felt for better footing, and fell heavily on his right side with a soft, cushioned swoosh, sending a shower of dry snow into the air. Once he tried to raise his head, then let it fall. As I came near I saw his chest heave out a mighty sigh, and one leg stiffen slightly. And then the woods were silent in the falling snow.

The open eye of the moose gazed blank and dull into the tree-stroked whiteness. A few wet flakes fell on the eyelids, melted on the warm nostrils, and sank into the long, unmoving ears.

The great, dark bulk was still. I felt, as I always do at such times, a strange and painful combination of emotions, if what one feels then can be called emotion precisely—a mingling of awe, of regret, of elation and relief. There was a quiet space in which to breathe, to acknowledge that something urgent and needed had been accomplished, all anxiety and uncertainty for the moment done with.

I returned down the snowy trail to the house to get my knife, my axe and saw, and a length of rope. And once more up the trail, I was soon at work on the carcass. First, I cut off the head with its heavy antlers. Then I tied a foreleg to a tree, and pushed and balanced the heavy, inert bulk onto its back. As always, it was strenuous work for a single man. But now death was forgotten. A transformation had taken place, and what had been a vital and breathing creature, capable of perception and of movement, was now only meat and salvage—a hairy mound of bone and muscle.

When I cut through the hide and strained inner tissue of the paunch, a cloud of red steam burst on the snowy air. And soon I could see deep into the steaming red cavity divided from the upper torso by the taut, muscular wall of the diaphragm. Working by feel alone in the hot soupiness of the rib cage, I loosened the windpipe, then pulled the stomach and the intestines clear, tumbling the heavy, stretched bag and ropy folds onto the snow. There was no fat on the veil nor around the kidneys, but I had not expected to find any. The meat would be lean, but it was better than no meat at all.

And now, with the entire inner part open to the light, I found that my single bullet had traveled the length of the body cavity, just under the spine, and had cut the blood vessels around the heart. Death had been swift, and little meat was spoiled.

That afternoon I dragged the quarters downhill through the snow and hung them on the rack behind the house. A week later a strong wind blew from the south, much of the snow melted, and a springlike warmth sailed through the woods. Where the killed moose had lain, the shaded snow thawed, then froze again, forming a kind of sunken circle that was stained pink and yellow, and matted with hair and leaves. It was soon to be covered by a fresh snowfall, and in a far month to come, to melt and be once more a part of the spring earth.

Ice

FOR SOME TIME NOW IN THE WOODS, away from the sun, in ravines and hollows where the ground is normally wet, the soil has darkened and is hard and cold to the touch. The deep, shaded mosses have stiffened, and there are tiny crystals of ice in their hairy spaces.

Water has sunk in the pools of the footpaths, in the high ridge trails the small potholes are ringed with transparent ice, or they are filled with whitened splinters shattered by the foot of some passing animal. Ice thickened with leaves surrounds a circle of open water in the flowing pool of the creek below the house.

The waters are freezing. From the reedy shallows outward to the centers of the roadside ponds: black ice, clear and hard, with bubbles that are white; opaque patches of shell ice that shatter easily when stepped on. The last ducks that kept to the open centers of the ponds are gone. Clumps of stiff dry grass stand upright there, held fast, casting their shadows on the evening ice.

Now that the steady frost has come, I have been thinking about the river. It is time to take a walk over the sandbars and islands, while there is still so little snow. It is late October; the smaller channels of this broad and braided river have long since stopped flowing, and their remaining pools are frozen. Far out in midriver, beyond the big, wooded island, a single large channel is now the only open water. The sound of that water, though distant, comes strong and pervasive over the dry land dusted with snow: a deep and swallowed sound, as if the river had ice in its throat.

One afternoon I take the steep path downhill to the riverbed. I make my way across to the big island over sandbar and dusty ice, past bleached piles of driftwood and through waist-high willows and alders, to the gravelly, ice-coated shore of the open channel. I walk a short distance out on the shore ice and stand there, looking at the water. A little wind comes down the wide river, over the frozen bars, smelling of winter.

Free of its summer load of silt, the water is clear in the shallows, incredibly blue and deep in the middle of the channel. Ice is riding in the water, big rafts of it crowding each other, falling through the rapids above me and catching on the bottom stones. Here where the current slackens and deepens, the water is heavy and slow with ice, with more and more ice.

Call it mush ice, or pan ice. It forms at night and during the colder days in the slack water of eddies and shallows: a cold slush that gathers weight and form. Drifting and turning in the backwater, it is pulled piecemeal into the main current and taken down.

Now on the heavy water great pans of ice are coming, breaking and reforming, drifting with the slowed current: shaggy doughnuts of ice, ragged squares and oblongs, turning and pushing against each other, islands of ice among lakes of dark blue water. Crowded shoreward by the current, they brush the shore ice with a steady "shsss" as they catch and go by. And with each sheering contact a little of that freezing slush clings to the outer edge of the shore ice. The ice is building outward, ridged and whitened, thickening with each night of frost, with each wave of shallow water that washes it.

As I look intently into the shallows, I see that boulder ice, a soft, shapeless and gluey mass, is forming on some large, rounded stones not far below the surface; the river is freezing from the bottom also. Now and then a piece of that water-soaked ice dislodges and comes to the surface, turning over and over. It is dirty ice, grey and heavy with sand, small stones, and debris.

Where it gathers speed in the rapids above, the sound of all this ice and water is loud, rough, and vaguely menacing. As the cold gradually deepens and the sunlight departs in the days to come, the floating ice will become harder and thicker, and the sound of its movement in the water will change to a harsher grinding and crushing. Now in the slowed current before me, it is mostly that steady and seething "shsss" that I hear, and underneath it a softer clinking as of many small glasses breaking against each other.

Standing here, watching the ice come down, I recall past years when I came to a channel much like this one, in mid-October with only an inch or two of snow on the gravel bars, to fish for salmon. I had with me a long pole with a steel hook at one end. Standing very still and quiet where the current slackened against the ice, I watched for the glowing red and pink forms of salmon on their way upriver in the last run of the season. Sometimes I caught sight of one toward midchannel, beyond reach of my pole; but often they traveled slowly along the edge of the ice, finning and resting, at times nearly motionless in the current. And carefully I extended my gaffhook along the ice edge behind the fish, and with a sudden, strong sweep and jerk I struck the fish through its body and flung it ashore.

The big hook made a nasty gash in the side of the salmon, and fish blood soon stained the snow where I piled them, one by one. If the fish happened to be a female heavy with eggs, the eggs sometimes spilled through the torn side of the fish, to lie pink and golden in the shallow snow with the glazed, mottled bodies of the freezing salmon.

There was something grand and barbaric in that essential, repeated act. To stand there in the snow and cold air toward the end of the year, with a long hook poised above the ice-filled river, was to feel oneself part of something so old that its origin was lost in the sundown of many winters: a feeling intensified, made rich by the smell of ice and cold fish-slime, by the steely color of the winter sky, and the white snow stained with the redness of the salmon: the color of death and the color of winter. And to all this was added the strong black of the ravens that gathered each evening as I was leaving the river, to clean the snow of the spilled eggs and blood.

I caught the big fish one at a time, watching and walking quietly along the edge of the ice, hour after hour. In a few days I had from two to three hundred salmon heaped in scattered mounds in the thin, dry snow of the sandbar, to be packed home a few at a time, heavy and frozen.

I see no salmon now as I stand here by this ice-filled channel, searching its green, bouldery shadows and bluer depths for a tell-tale flash of crimson. It may be that there is not a good run this fall, that I am too early or too late, or that the fish have taken another way upriver.

The sound of the water and the ice before me is one sound, familiar over the years. But there are other sounds of the ice, among them the strange and eerie moaning that comes from under the new ice of the pond when it is walked on, as if some sad spirit in the depth of the pond were trying to speak. In midwinter, a large sheet of ice will split with a rippling crack when the temperature suddenly changes or the ice bed shifts underneath, the ripple traveling fast with a winnowing sound at the end. And there are those small ticking sounds of the ice in the evening when the cold slides toward its deepest zero, as if a thousand hidden insects were chirping bitterly in chorus under the ice and snow. And, finally, the thundering crack and plunge of the shelf ice breaking off in the spring as the rising water wears away its support, a sound that can be heard for miles, like the detonation of a heavy building.

The ice sings, groans, howls, and whistles like a living thing. Years ago while hunting caribou in the Alaska Range, I heard the oldest lament of the ice. It was early in October, and the slow freeze was coming down over the empty land and its many lakes. As I stood alone and listening by the roadside one afternoon, I heard on the nearly windless air, as if from the earth itself, a muted and forsaken moaning from the lakes and ponds. It was a sound out of prehistory, of something deeply wounded and abandoned, slowly giving up its life to the cold. There were fleeting ghost-fires on the tundra, white-maned shadows from the bands of caribou fleeing before something I could not see. Then distant shots, gun-fire, the sound of a truck rattling by on the frozen road.

Here before me the river is still awake, still speaking in its half-choked mutter and murmur, still surging, pushing its ice-filled way across the open sand and gravel. But one day—it may be soon, or it may be very late, when the solstice sun clears the south horizon—the sound of all this surging and grinding, this shredding and crushing will stop. The great silence will have come, that other sound of the ice, which is almost nothing at all. This channel will have finally filled, the last open water will close, and the river will go under the ice. Snow will drift and cover the ice I stand on.

If I were to walk out here in midwinter, the only sound I would be likely to hear would be the wind, pushing snow across the ice. Only now and then, while walking over the frozen shallows, would I hear under my feet the sound of trickling water finding its way somehow through the ice. And later still, when ice has thickened to a depth of many feet on the deepest channel, I might hear far down in some snow-filled crevice the deep murmur and surge of the river running beneath me.

For the ice and the river under it are never still for long. Again and again throughout this long winter, water will find its way into the open, welling up from a seam in the ice, and spreading over the existing surface of ice and snow to freeze again in a perilous sheet. The wind will bring its dry snow to polish the new ice and turn it into a great slick and glare. Delicate flowers of frost will bloom upon it: small, glittering blossoms standing curled and fragile on the gritty ice, to be scattered by the first passage of air. And over the renewed expanse of ice there will be silence again, the silence of ice, unchanged since the first winter of Earth.

But all this is still to come, as it has come before. Winter is making its way across the land, over slope and plain, bog and high meadow, across lake and pond, outlet and feeder. It has progressed slowly this fall in an even, majestic tread, with a little more frost each night, a little less warmth each day. Meanwhile, the open water of the river flows at my feet, steady and heavy with ice, the deep sound of it filling the landscape around me.

I turn and walk back to the home shore whose tall yellow bluffs still bare of snow I can see nearly half a mile to the north. I find my way as I came, over dusty sandbars and by old channels, through shrubby stands of willows. The cold, late afternoon sun breaks through its cloud cover and streaks the grey sand mixed with snow.

As it has fallen steadily in the past weeks, the river has left behind many shallow pools, and these are now roofed with ice. When I am close to the main shore I come upon one of them, not far from the wooded bank. The light snow that fell a few days ago has blown away; the ice is polished and is thick enough to stand on. I can see to the bottom without difficulty, as through heavy, dark glass.

I bend over, looking at the debris caught there in the clear, black depth of the ice: I see a few small sticks, and many leaves. There are alder leaves, roughly toothed and still half green; the more delicate birch leaves and aspen leaves, the big, smooth poplar leaves, and narrow leaves from the willows. They are massed or scattered, as they fell quietly or as the wind blew them into the freezing water. Some of them are still fresh in color, glowing yellow and orange; others are mottled with grey and brown. A few older leaves lie sunken and black on the silty bottom. Here and there a pebble of quartz is gleaming. But nothing moves there. It is a still, cold world, something like night, with its own fixed planets and stars.

With an Axe and an Auger

I

THE OLD MAN LEANS FORWARD IN HIS CHAIR, listening. A car, a light truck, pounds by on the gravel road outside his cabin, and is gone. There is not much traffic here, over seventy miles from town, and each car that passes, coming down the long hill from the west, brings with it a new sound, a strangeness intruding on the quiet of the countryside.

Rarely, no more than once a week, a truck will stop, sound its horn, and drive on. It will be mail, or a box of groceries from town. Now there is only the swift surge of the engine and gears, the harsh grating of small stones under the tires, and silence again.

It is summer. Dust from the infrequent traffic, a fine grey powder, the soil of ten thousand years of ice, water, and wind, billows up in a heavy cloud and settles on the leaves of the alders and birches beside the road.

The old man relaxes. He settles his thin, stooped frame stiffly into his chair, and continues speaking to his visitor. His lined face is calm and reflective, resigned to the twilight before him.

He speaks once more of his younger days in the country, of the cabins he built, of his traplines, and of the people he knew—men and women who in one way or another left their mark on the country. He speaks briefly and affectionately of his wife, a native woman from one of the tribes in the region, famous as a sewer of skins. She has been dead three years.

132

He recalls the early settlement here, a mining camp once scattered along this creek and over the long hill to Richardson. At one time, and for less than a decade, there were perhaps a thousand people on the creeks and in the nearby hills. They were a population on the move, camped for a season or two to thaw and sluice the ground, to put together a town of logs, boards, and tin, and then too soon dispersed. Nothing of that remains but these pictures in the mind, and out in the wooded flats a couple of sunken cabins, a rotting sluicebox, a boiler slowly rusting, and the tailing piles, heaps of rounded stones overgrown by alders.

Now he is talking, picking his way with care among thoughts and words, glad to have someone to listen. Another time, older and frailer, he will sit by a lamp in that chair, reading and thinking. Summer will come, then fall, and winter again. His mind is drawn back onto old pathways. The woods grown up around him are filled with shadows. These shadows have names and faces, but only a few of them have voices, shaken like leaves in the wind. And farther on, leaving the darkness behind him, he comes to a lighted clearing.

Another man, well past middle age, old but still strong, is making bread. He stands tall and heavy at the table beside the big iron range. He dusts his board with flour and kneads the dough, pushing firmly upon it.

Now he pauses in his work and turns toward the window of his cabin. He peers through his eyeglasses out into the yard and to the woods beyond. He is watching for a moose. Last night he thought he heard one: a muffled hoof-crunch in the snow, the scrape of a birch bough, and his small dog barked.

It is November, winter is just beginning. He is alone, but he has grown used to being alone; his movements are those of a man accustomed to doing things for himself. When he speaks now and then, to himself or to his dog, his voice carries the strong accent of Sweden.

He makes two loaves from his lump of dough, and sets them to rise in pans on a shelf above the stove. From a bucket on the floor he dips water into a washpan and rinses his hands of flour. He carefully dries his hands on a piece of flour sacking, and when he is done, he covers the bread pans with the dampened cloth.

Now he bends down, opens the door of the range, and looks at the fire burning slowly on the grate. From a box on the floor beside the stove he chooses a sound, dry stick of birch and lays it upon the coals. The fire bed is deep and glowing, and the stick of birch flares into flame as its curled bark catches. Satisfied, he closes the door of the range and adjusts the draft.

He stands for a moment as if undecided. In these short days, what else to do? And then, having settled his mind, he takes a ragged wool jacket from the wall, a cap and mittens from a shelf, and turns toward the door of his cabin.

Well now, we might as well cut a little wood.

II

He was a man of medium height, straight and thin, dressed in wash-faded denim shirt and trousers, and wearing a weather-stained tan felt hat with a wide brim. He might have been a farmer a little seedy in his luck, an itinerant fieldworker, or simply a digni-fied hobo. He looked at me across the counter of the Fairbanks Economy Store with the eyes of an intelligent and half-trusting child. On the counter between us lay a well-worn army blanket, and he was holding out to me two silver dollars.

His name was Tom—if he ever gave a second name, I have for-gotten it. He was perhaps in his early seventies, with a beard in which the hairs were mingled yellow and white, roughly trimmed and curling on his cheeks. I knew him to be a longtime miner and prospector in the North, the familiar of one vanished camp or another. He was one of those who had never found substantial pay, or if he had, he had somehow wasted the money.

For some years now he had wintered in California and Ari-zona, working in the lettuce fields, picking potatoes and apples, and at intervals cooking in a diner to make his wages. Once more he had come back to the North. He had taken up a claim on one of the creeks in the Fairbanks district on ground that belonged to someone he knew. He was working at night in the North Pole Bakery, a block away from the store. By day he was putting together another outfit: stove, bedding, and tools. He was looking forward to the coming winter, and to one more spring on the creeks.

He came into the store every day or so for something he needed: a much-handled #2 shovel, a blunted pick that he claimed he could make as good as a new one. Or he came simply to talk, to pass the time with a few of the older men who gathered each morning in that cluttered and drafty warehouse of loose ends, to talk and spit and trade.

In his manner he was by turns animated and subdued. If he had any sort of audience, and the conversation got onto something he knew about, he'd pitch in with a remark or a story, his blue eyes flashing, his voice vibrant with an authority of the past. He knew, or seemed to know, the particulars of one district or another: Chandalar, Ruby, the Koyukuk, the name and district of an obscure river that emptied into the Beaufort Sea and from which he had once panned a little color. And then, at the edge of a sudden burst of talk, he fell silent again, as if he had drifted into some disconnection whose bounds and vacancies he alone knew.

He was not one of those wretched, cadging individuals, blurred with alcohol and caught up in the fantasies of a world that had never existed. He may have been left over from a day that was gone, finding only a tentative grasp on a present that had no real place for him, but he had that authority derived from the strict honesty of experience, and he asserted it on occasion with a directness you did not think to question.

My time then was divided between my job at the store in Fairbanks and a homestead I had taken up at Richardson, seventy miles upriver on the Valdez road. I would leave town late Friday afternoon and return in time for work on Monday. I came back to Fairbanks late one Sunday evening, having walked over thirty miles that day before I had caught a ride. The next morning, at work in the store, I was stiff and sore footed from my daylong hike in the hard-soled army shoes I had been wearing. I stepped painfully around the counter, complaining of the distance I had walked and of the lack of consideration from the drivers of the few cars and trucks that had passed me on the road.

Tom, who had come into the store and had overheard me, broke into a scoffing, good-humored laugh. "Why, you young people are mighty soft! We didn't think anything of walking thirty miles in a day when I was young. We did it all the time, packing a roadhouse on our backs besides!"

He turned to a couple of other men who were there and began to tell how he had walked the 160 miles from Fairbanks to Circle one spring, packing an outfit over Eagle Summit to prospect some ground he had staked the year before. That walk had taken him most of a week, but he made it. He stayed through the summer and caught a ride back downriver in the fall on the last boat of the season.

It was easy enough to believe him; he stood there, facing the high round bulk of the store's wood heater, and told about that walk with such a keen reliving of details, with an unrehearsed exactness. I saw that what I had taken as a hardship, as the personal unkindness of fate, had for him and his contemporaries been nothing more than the daily business of life. I was abashed, and I said no more about my forced march from Richardson.

Tom learned that I had the use of a truck, and on the strength of this he contracted with me to move his outfit to another location in town. He had been camping in the yard of an old Fairbanks house whose absentee owner had previously given him permission. But the house had recently been rented, and its new occupant had taken a dislike to the old man and by one comment or another had been prodding him to leave. So Tom had packed away, piece by piece, as much of what he owned as he could carry by himself. In doing so, he had strained his back, and there were still a few things he needed help with.

He came into the store one bright June morning to get me.

Business was slow, and I had already gotten permission to take an hour off. Tom and I left the store, got into the truck, and drove to an address on Third Avenue, a few blocks away. He was silent that morning, almost sullen, as if secretly aggrieved about something. He held onto the door handle of the truck cab, looking out the window at the traffic and the buildings we passed like someone who had never seen the like before. It was only Fairbanks, dusty and crowded, settling down again after the boom of the war years; but for him who had seen the place forty years before in the confusion and fire-loss of its beginnings, what he looked on that morning could as well have been the color and sound of an obscure market in central Asia.

We drove into an alley and stopped behind a ramshackle shed to the rear of a large frame house. Tom got down and opened a gate in the sagging wood fence. I backed the truck into the yard that was rank with uncut grass and last season's weed stalks. Stacked at the front of the shed was what remained of his outfit.

It was an odd assortment of things that included a threadbare carpet he had rescued from somewhere, and a thirty-gallon oil drum that he planned to make into a water barrel. There were a few lengths of salvaged lumber, some large sheets of cardboard, and half a dozen sides from packing cases whose thin slats he intended to use to line the walls of his tent for the winter.

As we were loading these things into the truck, a heavyset man in an undershirt and half-buttoned trousers came out the back door of the house. He looked at us for a moment, and called out in a rough voice that we were to be sure and take everything, he didn't want any junk left behind in his yard. Tom said nothing in reply and did not look in the man's direction. I felt the obscure tension between them. The plain annoyance in the man's voice spoke either of a justified resentment or of a habitual rudeness. But seeing that Tom was not alone, the man said nothing more. He watched us for a moment longer, and then went back indoors. In a short time we had everything loaded. I started the truck, and we drove out of the yard toward Tom's new campsite.

One of the churches in town had given him permission to camp on land that it owned near the Chena River in a part of town called Garden Island. His patched and weathered eight-by-ten-foot wall tent was pitched on bare ground a few yards from the water. A couple of lengths of new stovepipe poked at an angle through one side of the sloping canvas roof. On the ground in front of the tent there was a small rick of firewood.

I helped him unload the boards and the rest of his gear and pile it conveniently to one side of the tent. When this was done, I asked him if I could look inside. Moodily, he untied the flap at the entrance; I stooped down, half-crawled inside, and took stock of what I saw.

In one corner of the tent, near the entrance, was a small sheet-metal stove of the kind that prospectors and sheepherders have used for generations. It was set off the ground upon two large stones. Newspapers and kindling filled a shallow wooden crate on the near side of the stove; on the other side a similar box contained a couple of battered kettles, a frying pan, and assorted enameled metal dishes and cups.

Against the wall opposite the stove was a narrow mattress on which lay a folded blanket and a rolled sleeping bag. A few items of clothing hung from a string that was tied along the inside ridge of the tent roof.

The floor of the tent was dry sand mixed with gravel. The three-foot walls of grey canvas were half lined with packing boards similar to those we had brought that morning. Sunlight came through the canvas roof, outlining the seams and patches, and filling the tent with a subdued yellow light. Although the space was cramped and the headroom limited, it was summery and inviting in that soft light. In a far corner I saw a washtub, a gold pan, a pick, a shovel, an axe, and a bow-frame saw. Leaning upon a partly filled duffel bag was a well-used Model 99 Winchester carbine.

Everything was ordered and neat, the clothing washed and the bed made. Outside of the tent itself, and the packing boards, nearly the whole of what he owned could have been carried in a large wheelbarrow.

I pulled my head out of the tent and stood up. I was still very green; I had yet to spend a winter in the North, and I had recently absorbed many dire accounts of the previous winter, one of the coldest on record, with weeks of fifty below zero, of fuel shortages, frostbite, and cabin fever. I was preparing myself for hardships, with a substantial cabin in mind, and I was astonished that anyone could think of wintering in such a flimsy shelter as this was. I was without tact, and rather abruptly I said to Tom, "You mean you're going to spend the winter in this?"

Tom looked out across the Chena as if momentarily lost in the question I had asked him. He turned to me a face suddenly severe in its bewhiskered leanness, and with a kind of wounded defiance he said, "Shucks, you don't know anything. We were lucky sometimes to have this much, years back. Anyhow, it'll do."

I saw that without intending to I had in some way insulted him, and neither of us said more about it. He thanked me for my help and paid me three silver dollars from the small leather purse he carried. I got into the truck and prepared to go back to my job. As I drove off, I saw him bending over by his tent, arranging the pile of boards we had brought, his face turned away.

I learned little of his past, and nothing of his family, if he had one somewhere. It was tempting to think of him as somebody's lost grandfather, wandering the world in intermittent amnesia. More likely he was one of those eternal children who will never make a name or a fortune; a child of the weather, without complaint and harmless as a fly. He would never lose his innocence, no matter how badly the world behaved toward him. Disappointment would weather on him like the faded blue of his clothing, and he would go on in his quiet way, working and looking until death found him.

A week after helping him move, I quit my job and left town. I moved out to the homestead at Richardson, to build my cabin and spend my first winter alone. I saw Tom once more and briefly: he was crossing First Avenue on his way to the bakery, and I had no opportunity to talk to him. Whether he stayed through the summer there on the Chena, working at night and saving his money, or whether he moved out to his creek, I never knew. Late in the summer when I stopped at the store on one of my rare trips into town, no one spoke of him. He may have fallen ill and died that fall, one more name on a dwindling list; or he may have somehow made it through a last winter, camped in that thin, grey cotton tent, looking forward to another spring and whatever it was he still hoped to find.

<h1 style="text-align:center">III</h1>

He is a long way from Birch Lake now, two thousand miles and a little more. The distance is all the greater for being so much within him.

Here in this rain-swept city on Puget Sound he works in his brother's garden, trudging in a kind of sleep these last slow days of his life. And he whose best years were lived far north of here will pause sometimes and stand forgetful, like a man dazed by the sudden disappearance of familiar surroundings.

It is his brother who comes to the door and lets me in. He too is old, ruddy, and alert, retired long since from the lumber mill.

I enter the small front room of their house and see him standing there, a stocky figure grown slightly stouter in his waist. We greet each other, and I sense the momentary pause, the searching gaze in his pale blue eyes: Who is this, and from where? Do I know him? He isn't sure.

At first it is his brother who talks, filling the strangeness between us as well as he can. They don't see many people now. The brother's wife is dead, his children are grown and moved to other addresses, and the house is quiet. They are two old men whose paths long ago divided, but they have come together to finish out their lives. They are bound by blood, by the old ties of people who came from another country, and yet in some understandable way they are like strangers to each other.

They drink different brands of whiskey, and each of them goes to his own bottle when the time comes. Now it is afternoon, and someone has come to visit, an old friend and neighbor from the North.

The whiskey is brought from a cupboard, with stout, old-fashioned water glasses. He pours three inches of whiskey into a glass for me, no water or ice, and the same for himself. I watch his hands, thickened with work, the skin shining and translucent. It seems to me for a moment that they tremble slightly. No, they are steady.

We drink, and the warm liquor tastes strong and good. It's good to know, though scorned and damned by the saviors of humankind, that a few durable things can still be counted on: whiskey, the solace of the poor, the outcast, and the aging, the last religion.

"About all I do, drink and sleep!" he says, and we laugh about that. I know what he means.

He accepts me now. I am someone he used to know, though I see that he is still trying to fit my name and face to a map. The landscape is half obscured by mist, but somewhere within it there is a road by a river, high bluffs, and a mailbox on a post.

It is strange for me to find him here, so far from where I have been used to seeing him. It seems to me that there should be woodchips and straw on a plank floor, kindling and a pan of ashes by an iron stove. But the room is carpeted, neat and clean, and there is neither woodbox nor stove in the house.

He moves slowly and stiffly about the room, shuffling in a pair of slippers. He is dressed in the same tan workclothes I have seen him wear for years, as if he were ready once more to go out into the woods behind his cabin, or down to the lake for water, to stand looking across the quiet, sunlit surface to the birch hills on the far south shore.

From where I stand, I can see past an open door into his bedroom. A pair of trousers and a shirt lie folded on the seat of a chair; his shoes are neatly in place beneath it, and on the floor beside the chair a suitcase lies open as if he were packing to leave.

We sit down, finally, he in one chair and I in another. We talk, hesitating at first, groping among memories—of places, events, and people we both have known. The names, and the years brought with them, begin to awaken in him things he is forgetting here. I see the threads knitting in place as we talk.

There are some things I have wanted to verify, and so I ask him, remembering that once long ago he or someone else had told me. Whose cabin was it that burned down near Birch Lake one winter night over forty years ago? And who was it that had that long walk across the ice on frozen feet before he found shelter again?

"Oh, that was Jim Chisholm," he answers. "He was a big drinker!"

He remembers other things now, as he tries to respond to my questions. One thing follows another in no particular order: Who lived at what bend in the road, and whose was the place set back in the trees on the long grade above Woodchopper Hill? I learn once more that years ago in Fairbanks the teamsters would not harness the horses for work or travel in the winter if it was colder than forty below. That was the law.

"The horses, they freeze their lungs, or something like that." His voice is quiet and sure as he tells me this, knowing that's how it was.

I remind him how he and old Axel would come to Richardson at Christmas, bringing boxes of frozen whitefish they had netted under the Birch Lake ice. We all gathered around to look and marvel at the fat, good-eating fish glazed with ice. Good times, those days. Axel is long gone back to Michigan and has never written. Perhaps he is no longer living.

We drink, and light up a couple of cigarettes—it is something to do. As I watch him and listen to his searching phrases, I am reminded that he was always a gentle man. And for no reason, but because we have been talking about the woods, he says, "When I cut wood, I always look for a tree that is already hurt, got something wrong with it. I don't like to cut down a healthy tree. I think maybe they feel like we do."

He tells me this in such a way that I believe him, and there is nothing in it either odd or apologetic. He didn't like killing the mink he raised for many years up there on the lake. "I get attached to them, you know; kinda liked them."

He is restless and cannot stay seated in his chair. He crosses the room and picks up a newspaper from a table. There is some fact he wishes to verify in the day's news, and which he has been disputing with his brother. He was always one to be curious about the world and the nature of things, not easily content until he had squared the facts with his understanding.

Now, turning the pages and peering closely at the columns, he finds what he is looking for. Yes, here it is, just as I told you.

He puts the newspaper down, and stands as if momentarily turned from something he was to do. One of his shirtsleeves is partly rolled, and I see that the muscle in his forearm is shrunken; but he stands in his eighty years much as he used to. I don't know what he sees, looking inward that way.

"Hell to get old," he says finally, turning toward me, his eyes distant and baffled. No matter how trivial and how often said, it is true each time; especially for the man who has been used to working with his hands every day of his life, to walk and to be in the world.

I remember how we always found him when we came, alert and ready to talk, having read as well as he could the magazines that came his way, and the few borrowed books. English was not his native language, and even now his speech is sometimes thickened with an accent he has never shed completely. But with so much time alone in the long evenings and quiet days, even the simplest man might come to terms with himself and begin to perceive the world with some intelligence.

We would come to his big cabin set in the cleared slope above the lake; we came on foot across the spring ice, by boat in the summer, or by a long walk around the shoreline, through swamp and thicket. More often than not we found him at home, happy to see us, bringing his bottles of fresh beer up from the cellar beneath the floor almost before we had found a chair to sit in.

And so we would talk, while the home brew foamed in our glasses, and the firewood steamed and snapped in the range at the rear of the kitchen. The time went by as we reviewed the news, the local and the very distant: Who had come and who had gone? What was happening in the woods, along the road, and in the big world "out there"? The rabbits were few that year, but the moose looked good. The river had been high all summer, there were ducks on the lake. And as for the big world out there—for all the treaties and aggressions, things were pretty much the same. They don't change much, do they?

Something would be cooking while we sat there; or a ham was brought in and sliced, and fresh bread cut. Beer and smokes, as the afternoon sloped away into the long Northern dusk, the light that is never darkness; and everything around us seemed to fall into a kind of order unchanged for a thousand years.

He came to America from Switzerland in the early 1920s, following a brother and sister-in-law who had come over the year before. He left the old country to escape service in the Swiss Army, he said—a good enough reason. A job took him north, to Alaska, and that is where he stayed. One thing and another: a homestead on the lake southeast of Fairbanks, new friends, and a country he liked.

He was never married; so far as I know, he has never had a steady woman. I don't know why—shy, perhaps. But animals: the mink he farmed, and a dog that pulled his sled across the ice of the lake. When the dog got old and stiff, he pulled the load himself, the dog riding on the sled with the groceries.

And let's say that forty years went by at a slow and reasonable pace: one more summer in the woods, one more winter reading and cutting wood. He was an ironworker by trade, and he would sometimes take a job for the summer, in town or on one of the military bases farther north. But he always came back to the lake in the fall, rowing his heavy boat across the two miles of water, to his big, comfortable cabin in the meadow, his woodpile and small garden, the silence of the water and the woods.

And all that is gone, the land sold and the cabin empty. Sour-dock and fireweed have taken over the rhubarb patch and the meadow. Some things have changed, after all.

These will be the last, calm and empty years, with a watered garden, a trimmed lawn, a little money in the bank. It will be enough finally to sit in the house day and evening, while the last strength goes, looking into the distance from whatever window he finds himself beside.

We have more whiskey and feel the good glow in our bellies. His brother has gone into the kitchen to make sandwiches for us; he is friendly and obliging, but his thoughts come from another world than ours.

"Look there, now," the brother says to us from the kitchen. "There's a fire across the sound. It looks like a big house or a factory burning."

We all stand at the kitchen window, looking at a brightness across the water, an orange blaze that wavers and intensifies on the Canadian coast. In a moment, I see that it is only the setting sun reflected in those distant windows. It looks like a fire, hot and molten, but it isn't. I don't tell them this; it's a lot more fun to think that there might really be a fire over there.

"It's a big one for sure."

"Wonder what it is?"

"Well, we'll read about it in the paper tomorrow, I guess."

The excitement is soon over. We sit at the kitchen table and eat our sandwiches. We eat in silence for a while, and then begin to talk again. A familiar calm is present, now that I think of it, something of the old, quiet routine, though it is colored with sadness.

It will be time for me to leave pretty soon. I delay, thinking that we may not see each other again. There is so much we have known together, but the years are carrying us away from the old, firm landmarks. We stand before a certain window, gazing into some far place. There is a fire there, warmth, and people we know. The names there have always fitted the things we could see and touch. This is the world we know, and we know ourselves as part of it.

And something happens. It happens slowly, but as surely as the sun comes back each spring and leaves us again in the fall. One more old face has vanished; another, younger and stranger, is in its place. Imperceptibly, the world grows distant, as if one's sight were failing as he watched. Thoughts, physical movements struggle to hold their places, then give way and reassemble in a different order. We learn to live with spaces and silences we had not known before.

Memory, something we had relied on above everything else. Like a boat untied from the shore, that faculty, too, leaves us: the days blur together, we are borne too far to see. We are alone, confused among shadows; there are no known voices, and we feel around us, probing and insistent, the cold cramp of death. Now sleep is the one possible thing. Night and the earth are waiting.

And then, in that shadowy place, to be recalled by a name, a voice, a face; and for a brief time light flickers upon a few images we understand. We are home again, and the known words come to our lips, to be heard and shared by a listener.

I stand and drain my glass. It is getting late, and finally I have to leave. He follows me down the steps and across the lawn. I can see that he is still trying to fit all the pieces together, to make sense of the things we've been saying. But he seems awake and happier now, his mind once more lighted and clear.

We say good-bye, and grasp each other's hand. His brother has come to the porch of the house; he stands there, apart and smiling. Come back again. It's good to visit.

He stands there on the lawn in the dusk, looking after the car as I drive away. I will not forget the affectionate, the still-strong grip on my arm when we parted. He *does* remember; I think now he always will. It's good to know.

IV

The land lives in its people. It is more alive because they worked it, because they left this hillside and that creek bottom marked by their shovels and axes. The meaning of this place lies in the rough weight of their hands, in the imprint of their gum-booted travel.

Here among the willows you will find old pipe fittings, valves, and chunks of steam hose; they are scattered with rusty tins, bent hoops, and splintered boxes. In this place, Ike Isaacson sank his prospect hole and fired his boiler. His cabin has fallen to rot and rain, but for those of us who remember, this tangled blueberry flat is still Ike's bench.

Up there where the woods are thinned, someone whose name has escaped all memory built his cache and hung up his winter's meat. Lying there, half-sunken in the moss, are the hewn and punky timbers, and here in the living spruce a rusty spike has gathered a knot of pitch.

And on this sandy knoll, someone else we knew had a cabin. Here were the fence posts of his garden. And look, a few woody stalks of rhubarb still break through the sod by the corner post each spring.

At this bend in the road, not far from the fallen bridge, Melvin killed his grizzly with a pistol.

They are useful ghosts, these old inhabitants with their hand-worn implements, their settled lives. They tell us something of what we have been, and if we live long enough and well enough, what each of us may become: one more sign of our residence on earth, alive by reason of remembered love.

I was lucky to have known them when I did, for they are no longer standing in their patched wool and mended cotton. In some way I have always accepted, they were my people, if the phrase now means anything, and the best of them I have loved with a deep appreciation that has never left me. They were friends and teachers, and I do not expect to see their kind again.

When I think of them now, it is of something hugely tender and forgiving, akin to a healing thingness in the world that assures the soil of its grasses, the earth of its sun.

They are voices, gestures, faces peering out of old photographs, but not that only. They live as names spoken from the shadows: Campbell, Melvin, Hershberger, Doherty, Fry. There were some, like Kievic and Sam Loma, who died before I came; I knew them only as figures looming half legendary in the local stories.

The cemetery site at Richardson long ago caved into the Tanana; it is silt and driftwood with the rest of the riverbed. On a slope outside Fairbanks, intergrown with the birches, with mosses and strawberry vines, the glass-covered nameplates are cracked and muddied, their letters erased by the weather. No doubt they are all recorded in some basement file in the courthouse, written down with the deeds and taxes in a musty ledger.

But the people live in these hills, in the shape of their ditches, their mounds and cellars. They are accounted for in the names they gave to the country, to its furrows and pockets, its upraised bones; a hidden lake, a creek like so many others, one windy dome among a hundred ridges. I know of more than one high tributary named in passing by a man reminded of the place he came from; amused or forgetful, inventing as he walked, or moved perhaps by something in the far-off news of that day: *Empire, Republican, Buckeye, Carrie Nation.*

A wandering spirit came home to the land. In the shape of a man, it cleared a space in the forest and built a shelter from the trees at hand. It came to learn the ways of this country; to sleep and awaken, to flourish and grow old; to watch the river, the clouds moving east, the frost in the grass.

It will never die completely. Look for it in the trails you follow, in the amber blazes on black bark. You will find it in the settled forge, in the rotting windlass, in the cabin sill you come upon by a creek that has no name; in the green scar on that far hill.

Shadows

I

THERE ARE SHADOWS OVER THE LAND. They come out of the ground, from the dust and the tumbled bones of the earth. Tree shadows that haunt the woodlands of childhood, holding fear in their branches. Stone shadows on the desert, cloud shadows on the sea and over the summer hills, bringing water. Shapes of shadow in pools and wells, vague forms in the sand-light.

Out of the past come these wind-figures, the flapping sails of primitive birds with terrible beaks and claws. Shadows of things that walked once and went away. Lickers of blood that fasten by night to the veins of standing cattle, to the foot of a sleeping man. In the Far North, the heavy, stalled bodies of mastodons chilled in a black ooze, and their fur-clad bones still come out of the ground. Triceratops was feeding in the marshlands by the verge of the coal-making forest.

Shadows in doorways, and under the eaves of ancient buildings, where the fallen creatures of stone grimace in sleep. Domestic, wind-tugged shadows cast by icy branches upon a bedroom window: they tap on the glass and wake us. They speak to the shadows within us, old ghosts that will not die. Like trapped, primordial birds, they break from an ice pool in the heart's well and fly into walls built long ago.

Stand still where you are—at the end of pavement, in a sun-break of the forest, on the open, cloud-peopled terrace of the plains. Look deeply into the wind-furrows of the grass, into the leaf-stilled water of pools. Think back through the silence, of the life that was and is not here now, of the strong pastness of things— shadows of the end and the beginning.

It is autumn. Leaves are flying, a storm of them over the land. They are brown and yellow, parched and pale—Shelley's "pestilence-stricken multitudes." Out of an evening darkness they fly in our faces and scare us; like resigned spirits they whirl away and spill into hollows, to lie still, one on the other, waiting for snow.

II

I stepped out into my yard on a warm October evening, just before dark. I forget now why I had gone out—perhaps for an armload of wood, or to check on the last of the sunset and the oncoming night sky. In those days, when I was done with eating and sleeping, the natural place for me to be was outdoors.

I hadn't been out long when I saw what at first I thought was a large, dark leaf blowing toward me in the dusk. But there was no wind. Like a silent and tumbling leaf it brushed by me and disappeared behind the house. Moments later it returned, darting erratically overhead, and again it dropped from sight, this time down the road toward the river. It occurred to me that it might be a late swallow, but it seemed too dark, silent, and strange, and so far as I knew all swallows had long since left the country.

Again the strange visitor fluttered past me in the semidarkness. And suddenly I knew that this swift, wayward, climbing and falling thing was a bat, that there must be more than one flying in the dusk around me. As the fall evening slowly edged into night, I stood still and watched.

It was impossible to keep track of them in that dim light. As soon as I had one fixed in flight against the sky, it veered off into the darkness of the trees and vanished. The bats flew with a queer, jerky movement—a flight somewhat like that of a butterfly, but stronger and swifter. It was as if, out of the still evening air in which they flew, a sudden and unfelt gust of wind snatched them aside; or that at any moment they felt the limit of an invisible string that yanked them from their path.

I knew nothing of bats. Never before had one come to the yard, and never in many evening walks to the river had I seen a bat near the water. I knew only this swift, buoyant flight in the dusk, the mysteriousness of their late appearance in a country from which all other summer creatures had gone. In a kind of spell I watched them for as long as I could distinguish any movement in the darkness. The fall night closed over the landscape, leaving a few stray gleams of light on the river, and I went back indoors.

Looking among the nature guides on the bookshelf, I found a section on bats and began reading. I learned that the earliest fossil bat has been dated back to the Eocene, ninety-five million years after the first bird flapped through the Jurassic skies, and long after the last flying reptiles had become part of the earth's stone history. The teeth and skulls of fossil bats are similar to those of early monkeys, suggesting a common ancestor. And the writer went on to say that bats may be among our earliest relatives.

Only two kinds of bats were found in the Far North, and in Alaska these were thought to inhabit a region two or three hundred miles farther south. But obviously that information was incorrect. I soon decided, from my reading and from what I had been able to observe of their size and flight habits, that the bats I had seen were the *Little Brown myotis,* one of the smallest and commonest of North American bats. They belonged to a widespread family of insect-feeding bats, having a body no larger than that of a meadow mouse, with a wingspread of perhaps ten inches. I read that they were colonial in their habits; that some individuals hibernated during the winter, while others migrated; that they slept by day in caves, in old buildings and hollow trees. In deep dusk they could be seen flying near water and at the edge of the forest. And what I was reading seemed to be true, for here they were, hunting my cleared spaces among the birches.

The next evening I walked up the highway to the mailbox to post a letter. Again the evening was still and warm, with an occasional light air moving over the hills and a deep gold light on the river channel in the southwest. I soon saw a bat flying up and down the roadway, back and forth, swiftly changing altitude in pursuit of the insects that were still abroad. More than once it vanished among the trees bordering the roadside, to reappear as a tumbling, leaf-shaped thing against the clear night sky.

It seemed to me as I walked, my attention held by the constant surprise of its flight, that the bat in turn was attracted by my passage on the road. It brushed by me, and abruptly out of the hovering darkness it swooped over my head and flew before me up the road. I felt oddly comforted, exhilarated by the nearness of this unique and searching creature in the dusk. When I returned from the mailbox, the bat again seemed to accompany me—as if, in obedience to some obscure purpose in life, it too delighted in the companionship.

The warm weather held for another day or two, and then with that swiftness of deepening fall the days and nights turned cold. I did not see the bats again that year.

Thinking on their sudden appearance and swift departure, I wondered where they had gone. Had they really flown south, far south, carried aloft by that delicate membrane stretched between wrist and foot? It seemed to me unlikely that they could pass the mountains through Canada, or survive the coastline and the stormy Gulf. Even so, I imagined them making their way somehow, flitting from corridor to corridor, dependent on the insects still awake in that uncertain latitude.

Or had they found a crevice in a nearby rock face, some earth-warmed cavern, and deep in that shelter drawn in upon themselves whatever warmth their small bodies possessed, and gone to sleep for the winter?

I was not to know the answers to my questions. As the days shortened, I thought of the bats from time to time, wondering what it would be like to be with them, wherever they were, clinging head-down in sleep to a precarious edge, waiting for spring— perhaps to freeze and never awake.

"Bats have few enemies. Bad weather is one of them. When not hibernating, they seem unable to endure long fasts; protracted cold, windy, rainy weather that keeps insects from flying, causes considerable mortality. . . ."*

For the rest of us plodding terrestrial creatures, snow came soon, and the year plunged deeper into frost.

The following year in late September I hiked down into Banner Creek from Campbell's Hill on my way home from hunting. Halfway down the open hillside I stopped briefly to look inside a dilapidated frame shack left behind by miners a few years before. It was nearly dusk, and the light inside the shack was poor. But as my eyes became accustomed to the gloom, I found that I was not alone in the shack. My attention was caught by a dark, rounded shape on the wall near a window, halfway up from the floor. I stepped quietly over to it and found a small brown bat clinging to a crack in one of the boards. I had no light with me, and I was unable to see clearly any details of the creature, but it seemed to me that it was awake and that a pair of bright, steady eyes was watching me. I had a momentary impulse to pick the bat up and carry it outside where I could have a better look at it. I decided not to disturb it. I might have learned more, but I felt that it would not be worth the risk of scaring or injuring the bat.

After a brief search of the bare room, and finding no other bats, I left the shack and quietly shut the door. The door had been closed when I came, and the bat had apparently entered through a hole in the eaves or by a broken windowpane.

A week and some days later a pair of bats once again came to the homestead yard on a mild evening and flew about, as they had the year before, until long after dark. And again, when the period of warm evenings ended, they disappeared.

They visited the homestead in this way for about four years.

---

* Henry Hill Collins, Jr., *Complete Field Guide to North American Wildlife.*
Harper & Brothers, New York, 1958, p. 267.

They came once or twice in late summer, but more often in the fall when a south wind had blown the last leaves from the birches, when the woods were silent and waiting. That rare, mild evening came, a few insects—moths and gnats—emerged, and the dusk took on its brief summer life again.

Then, as mysteriously as they had first appeared, the bats deserted the homestead. I do not remember having seen them before that time, and not often since. During that same four-year period there were scattered reports of bats seen near Fairbanks in the evenings by people who did not know they existed so far north. It is likely that in milder years since then these small bats have come and gone in other neighborhoods, mostly unnoticed by people in lighted houses.

It may have been that from time to time a change in the climate of the Interior, so slight that it was otherwise unmarked, extended their range northward; or that a subtle shift in the pattern of their local migration brought them to the river, to the yard and the open field above it. And then, like so many other events in our lives, perhaps no explanation is required. A wind from a great, hidden tree blew in our direction one evening and, like leaves loosened from a shaken bough, they came and they vanished.

Despite the shadowy undertones of folk literature and old wives' tales—the imagery of fear and transformation, of witchcraft and brooms, and despite what I remembered from childhood of my mother and grandmother's alarm at the very thought of having a bat in the house—I have never felt uneasiness in their presence. I remember an incident years ago when I was a student in Washington. I came home late one night to the rooming house where I lived; as I climbed to the landing on the second floor I saw a large bat flying up and down the corridor. It flew swiftly, avoiding me each time it passed. The midfall evening was warm, and the bat may have been attracted by the moths that were fluttering at the landing light. I was concerned that the bat would be trapped and injured, and before going upstairs to my room I opened a window at one end of the corridor.

"They are not witches. . . . They will not try to get into your hair. Like most animals and some people, what they want is to be left alone."*

Although surely indifferent to our presence, as all wild things tend to be, they seemed to me in that Far Northern place, at the uttermost limit of their range—remote from attics and belfries, from all folklore and superstition; remote from every human infringement that has so often determined the existence of their kind—to be warm, curious, and friendly creatures whose lives momentarily touch our own.

Another and distant fall shed its leaves in the wind; no bats came, and something of that rare kinship was missing in the October evening.

III

I speak much of twilight, of dusk and evening. I began with shadows and I must end with them, having lighted a clearing along the way. To go further is to describe a persistence of the forest and its shadows within us. How the man-beast of fantasy and star-crossed resemblance returns, as dream image clothed in scales, feathers, and fur; in those confused reaffirmations of transitional life— werewolves and vampires, blood-drinking night-things with sharp teeth and pointed ears.

The imagery of early art and literature is rich in representations of men who have put on the hair and strength, the fierceness and courage, of the lion, bull, and bear, the fleetness of the deer, and the eyesight of the eagle. Related figures, ranked in the lower orders of fox and ferret, assume characteristics of deceit and thievish cunning. Bats displayed on the coats of arms of old families in Britain were meant to show traits of watchfulness and wakefulness. A bat emblem signified a man of quick and secret execution.

A debased form of this identification speaks to us today in the vocabulary of the sports pages, in the labels distributed among

---

* Ibid., p. 298.

items of manufacture, in the names often given to weapons of warfare to suggest a threatening and fearless aspect; and in those comic but predatory cartoon figures of batmen and wolfmen who flourish in the atmosphere of another, more fantastic planet where the mind roams at will among inherited images.

Examples of blood-identity, of remedies and safeguards, cram the histories. An ancient proverb concerning madness tells us that "he who eats the heart or tongue of a bat shall flee from water and die." A bat tied to the left arm will keep away sleep. A bat carried three times around a house and nailed head-down above the doorway will bar misfortune. The heads of young bats and swallows, pounded and mixed with honey, will improve dim vision. And if you should be so fortunate as to see anything hidden, submerged in darkness, anoint your face with the blood of a bat, and you may read by night.

An early explorer in Australia was warned not to kill a bat, for it was "brother belonging to black fellow." In colonial Mexico an old woman one day complained to two priests of their abuse of her. When in astonishment they protested, she reminded them that the day before they had chased a bat from their house. "I was that bat," the old woman said, "and now I am exhausted."

Lodged in batlore are the souls changed by sleep, who are never seen in daylight when men are awake. So, in deposits of slate fifty-million-years old, lie the remains of fossil bats, sound in their stony sleep, who will awaken when the oceans rise and unending night claims the earth.

Somewhere in Christian folklore the story is told of how Jesus, retired to seclusion in the mountains and cut off from a view of the desert, made a clay image of a winged creature and breathed upon it. And immediately it opened its wings and fled into a cavern in the mountains. Thereafter it emerged every night at sunset to tell him of the close of day.

The Maya Kingdom of Darkness was ruled by Camazotz, the death-bat. Representations show the god in human form with batlike wings, the nose-leaf shaped to a stone knife with which he slays his victims. A stream of blood flows from the god's mouth to signify the destruction of life and devouring of darkness.

An outpouring of images, as numerous, as filled with voices as a colony of bats issuing from a desert cave on its nightly search. The awakened bats swarm above the thorn-brush, and in the steep light of dusk an echo comes back to us ten million years after the sound was uttered and the mouth is dust.

Before knowledge there was wisdom, grounded in the shadows of a dimly lit age. We ourselves have been night creatures, and once the human soul left its sleeping body, to soar and feed night-long in the shape of a bat or exotic bird, returning to the sleeper at daybreak.

Turn out all the lights in your town or city, and see how swiftly life returns to the shadows, how soon from within unlit trees and from silent doorways the ancient dread comes back, and night is once more filled with snouts and whispers, with leathery wings, and heavy bodies colliding.

The attitudes flicker and change, rehearsed continually on the screen of the wind. To be merely a creature on earth, to be left alone in an acre of grass, has seldom been sufficient—not since man the hunter scanned the open fairway, crouched in ambush, and took passionately to himself the skins of killed beasts, tore their meat from the bones, drank their milk and blood, and then by torchlight traced their outlines on a high rock face in soot and ochre.

As if fed by necessity, by intuition that blood indeed moves the sun, and is the sun's energy reddened and intensified in the human heart, imagination chooses its victims in an act of perpetual sacrifice. It seizes upon the wild creature and turns it into an image of some interior force we feel but cannot see, be it god or demon.

It is as though we require that evil exist, and that we find its faces in the world. A potential harm animates the expressions of certain animals—a menace in the wet lips drawn back on the gleaming teeth, as in the strange, thirsty little muzzles of bats and shrews. So a silent terror accompanies the predatory armor and clicking mandibles of beetles—all that, in the grass world beneath us, in the water world and leaf world around us, signifies the relentless stalking of an insect prey.

In spite of all subsequent knowledge, the outcome of "objective," "detached" observation, something fixed in the soul finds satisfaction in these images of cunning and ferocity. We respond to a sound in the syllables of certain words and phrases: "the Wolf of the Air, and the Wolf of the Pond." The grimaces, the frozen smiles, the wind-snarls of the spirit-faces cut into the eroding stone of temples and stelae, contain our loves, our hates, and our angers. In that mysterious logic of totemic art, the monstrous carved and painted guardians posted before the law and the household preserved for those within a precarious peace.

We misread these images if we think of them as horrible and frightening only, for the harm they seem to threaten. For behind that immediate and apparent violence they are as well, and perhaps above all, images of a lost and intenser being. Standing erect in polished bronze, Yamakanda, a many-armed Tibetan god, clutches his consort in what appears to be a ferocious and devouring embrace. But that embrace can be understood as an expression of devotion and love, and the terrible, wrinkling smile that accompanies it is formed with the only face the beast-god has to wear.

And still that lost being pursues us, no matter how remote and abstract our sensibilities have become. The mark of the forest is on us, never to be burned away. Upon the capitals of pillars in the chapterhouses of old churches in Europe the staring likenesses of lords and kings have been carved, their foreheads clenched and bitten by swine-headed creatures, by harpies and scaled dragons whose taloned and beaked reality often seems more real than any clinical terms we can assign to pain, disorder, and sorrow. In the final canto of Dante's *Inferno*, Satan appears as a huge, half-frozen batlike being whose wings, opening and closing, fan a great frost and send forth the world's evil. A lasting grief rolls down those towering and blackened features in tears of ice.

And then, released from an old grip of terror, and with nothing but the familiar woodland of rain, leaf, and sunlight to walk through, the haunted, legendary features dissolve, and we see only another being on earth—a bounding bundle of red fur, a burst of grey feathers—as bound to necessity as ourselves.

And of the bats at Richardson, whose brown leaf-shapes crossed the twilight at such rare intervals, to speak now and then of companionship and delight is sufficient, for these may be found anywhere in the pure act of being, of pursuing one's way of daylight and dusk, filling by right that clearing, that space of air, that acre of soil and grass, undeflected by regret or thought of tomorrow.

The weather changes, the ice retreats or advances; drought and rain alternate as the continents slide and the chill vectors shift north or south. The woods vanish before the axe, the saw, and the plow; they reappear when the handgrip relaxes. Shadows disperse to the outskirts of our lighted settlements, and the heavy smoke-dimmed dusk is voiceless.

I walk by the roadside, looking into the strong west light. The air is warm and the wind is gentle. A late swarm of gnats blows up from somewhere in the roadside brush. They hover before me, give way and reassemble behind me. They remind me of past evenings, of shadows, whispers, and vanished companions. However things may be elsewhere in this calm autumn world, there are no bats flying above the roadway this evening.

And to think, from this long vista of empty light and deepening shade, that so small and refined a creature could fill an uncertain niche in the world; and that its absence would leave not just a momentary gap in nature, but a lack in one's own existence, one less possibility of being.

As if we were to look out on a cherished landscape, hoping to see on the distant, wrinkled plain, among the cloud shadows passing over its face, groups of animals feeding and resting; and in the air above them a compact flock of waterfowl swiftly beating its way to a farther pond; and higher still, a watchful hawk on the wind. To look, straining one's eyes, noting each detail of lake, meadow, and bog; and to find nothing, nothing alive and moving. Only the wind and the distance, the silence of a vast, creatureless earth.

Richardson: The Dream

I T IS NIGHT IN MIDWINTER on the Richardson road. Snow is falling, and there is snow on the roadway. The road is narrow and winding, brushed in on either side by birches and willows whose branches cross each other, heavy with snow. The right-of-way has not been cleared for many years.

A light wind blowing out of Delta sweeps the flakes along; they fall on the unmarked roadway. No cars have passed for hours and days, not for many weeks. It has been snowing for a long time. The snow is light and dry, the kind of snow a man may walk through, the snow blowing aside in his passage.

The figure of a man approaches, walking west on the road, toward Richardson. He is bundled in a loose and baggy parka, in the style men used to wear, an outer garment like a shell, worn to break the wind.

He comes on past the old Doherty cabin, pushing aside the loose and drifting snow as he walks. He peers before him into the darkness. It may be Hans. No, it is Melvin. Perhaps, then, it is Hershberger—he would be walking from that direction; it would be he, of course. We cannot tell. His face is hidden within the hood of his parka. A stranger, and yet he knows his way.

The roadhouse looms before him in the snow-filled darkness. There are no lights there anywhere, not in the house nor in the yard. There is no smoke from the chimney; a little snow lies crusted on the cap of the stovepipe.

He mounts the open porch, kicking snow from the steps. He

161

stands before a door, he knocks and listens. There is no sound in answer; no dog barks, no light comes on within.

He goes to one of the tall windows, leans there and looks inside, his forearm resting on the framing. He knocks again on the glass.

The old logs of the building are dusted with snow; there is snow in all the cracks and snow on the sills. Snow lies deep on the roof, and there is no sheet of ice to hang heavy and gleaming from the eaves; there has been no fire in that house for a long time. No one is home.

The man stands on the porch and listens. The rough and peeling signboard creaks on its wires overhead. There is no other sound but the wind, quiet with snow in the forest. No stars can be seen, there are no lights anywhere in the distance. The entire landscape seems dark and empty, the vast Interior a place of snow and silence.

The man turns away, pulling his parka hood around him. He walks again on the road in the direction he came from, into the wind, toward Tenderfoot Hill. He disappears in the darkness. Snow closes around him, filling his tracks as he goes.

About the Author

JOHN HAINES, poet, essayist, and teacher, was born in 1924, in Norfolk, Viginia. After studying painting in Washington, D.C. and New York City, he homesteaded, from 1954 to 1969, in Alaska, at Mile 68, Richardson Highway, southeast of Fairbanks. Mr. Haines is the author of numerous collections of poems and critical essays, among which the most recent are *Fables and Distances, New and Selected Essays* (1996); *A Guide to the Four-Chambered Heart* (1996); *The Owl in the Mask of the Dreamer, Collected Poems* (1993, expanded paperback edition 1996); and a memoir, *The Stars, The Snow, The Fire* (1989). A collection of early poems, *At the End of This Summer: Poems 1948–54,* was published by Copper Canyon Press in 1997.

In addition to two Guggenheim Foundation Fellowships for poetry and a National Endowment for the Arts Fellowship previously granted, Mr. Haines received a Literary Award in 1995 from the American Academy of Arts & Letters, and, in 1996, he was guest lecturer at the Annual Summer Wordsworth Conference in Grasmere, England. Recent academic appointments include those at Ohio University, George Washington University, and the University of Cincinnati. He occupied the Chair in Creative Arts at Austin Peay State University in Tennessee in 1993, and, in 1997, he was awarded the Annual Fellowship of the Academy of American Poets.

Mr. Haines lives in Helena, Montana, with his wife, Joy.

The Stars, the Snow, the Fire was set in Adobe Caslon, a face drawn by Carol Twombly in 1989, and based on the work of William Caslon (c. 1692–1766), an English engaver, punchcutter, and typefounder.

This book was designed by Wendy Holdman, set in type by Stanton Publication Services, Inc., and manufactured by Bang Printing on acid-free paper.

Graywolf Press is dedicated to the creation and promotion of thoughtful and imaginative contemporary literature essential to a vital and diverse culture. For further information, visit us online at: *www.graywolfpress.org*.

Other Graywolf titles you might enjoy:

Kabloona: Among the Inuit by Gontran de Poncins
Owning it All by William Kittredge
An Autobiography by Edwin Muir
From the Island's Edge ed. by Carolyn Servid
The Way It Is by William Stafford
The Saddest Pleasure: A Journey on Two Rivers
    by Moritz Thomsen